THE TRAINS LONG DEPARTED

Ireland's Lost Railways

THE TRAINS LONG DEPARTED

Ireland's Lost Railways

TOM FERRIS ∿

Gill & Macmillan

Gill & Macmillan Ltd
Hume Avenue, Park West, Dublin 12
with associated companies throughout the world
www.gillmacmillan.ie

978 07171 4785 4

Index compiled by Cover to Cover
Cartography by Stephen Johnson
Typography design by Make Communication
Print origination by O'K Graphic Design, Dublin
Printed and bound in the UK by MPG Books Ltd,
Cornwall

This book is typeset in 13/16 pt Minion.

The paper used in this book comes from the wood pulp
of managed forests. For every tree felled, at least one
tree is planted, thereby renewing natural resources.

A CIP catalogue record for this book is available from
the British Library.

5 4 3 2 1

CONTENTS

LIST OF ABBREVIATIONS

B&CDR	Belfast & County Down Railway
BC&RB	Ballymena, Cushendall & Red Bay
BER	Baltimore Extension Railway
B&NCR	Belfast & Northern Counties Railway
BTC	British Transport Commission
B&W	Bagenalstown & Wexford
C&B	Cork & Bandon Railway
CB&SCR	Cork, Bandon & South Coast Railway
CofDSPCo	City of Dublin Steam Packet Company
C&H	Chester & Holyhead
CIÉ	Córas Iompair Éireann
C&KJR	Cork & Kinsale Junction Railway
C&KR	Cork & Kinsale Railway
DART	Dublin Area Rapid Transport
D&BJR	Dublin & Belfast Junction Railway
D&CDR	Downpatrick & County Down Railway
D&D	Dublin & Drogheda
D&E	Dundalk & Enniskillen
D&G	Dundalk & Greenore
D&K	Dublin & Kingstown
DN&G	Dundalk, Newry & Greenore
D&SER	Dublin & South Eastern Railway
DW&W	Dublin, Wicklow & Wexford
FVR	Finn Valley Railway

GJR	Grand Junction Railway
GL&M	Great Leinster & Munster
GNR	Great Northern Railway
GNRB	Great Northern Railway Board
GSR	Great Southern Railways
GS&WR	Great Southern & Western Railway
GWR	Great Western Railway
IÉ	Iarnród Éireann
IR	Irish Rail
INWR	Irish North Western Railway
IOC	Irish Omnibus Company
ISER	Irish South Eastern Railway
IVR	Ilen Valley Railway
KJR	Killarney Junction Railway
L&BER	Letterkenny & Burtonport Extension Railway
L&E	Londonderry & Enniskillen
L&LSR	Londonderry & Lough Swilly Railway
LMS	London, Midland & Scottish
L&NWR	London & North Western Railway
LR	Letterkenny Railway
MGWR	Midland Great Western Railway
MR	Midland Railway
NCC	Northern Counties Committee
N&E	Newry & Enniskillen
N&G	Newry & Greenore
NIR	Northern Ireland Railways
NIRTB	Northern Ireland Road Transport Board
P&D	Portadown & Dungannon
RMS	Royal Mail Ship
RPSI	Railway Preservation Society of Ireland

SL&NCR	Sligo, Leitrim & Northern Counties Railway
SWR	South Wales Railway
U&C	Ulster & Connaught
UR	Ulster Railway
UTA	Ulster Transport Authority
WC&DJR	Wexford, Carlow & Dublin Junction Railway
WCR	West Cork Railway
W&L	Waterford & Limerick
WL&W	Waterford, Limerick & Western
WNR&W	Waterford, New Ross & Wexford
WWW&D	Waterford, Wexford, Wicklow & Dublin

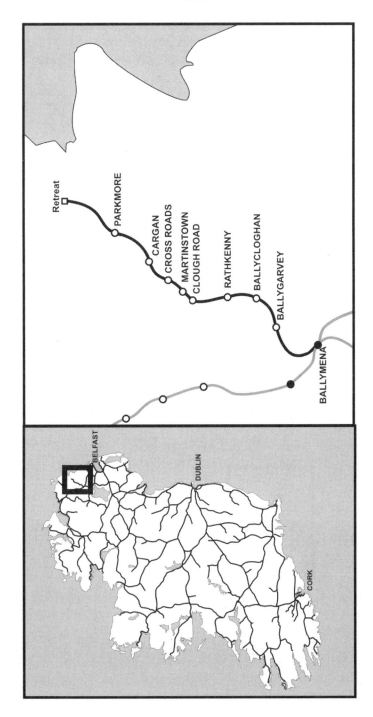

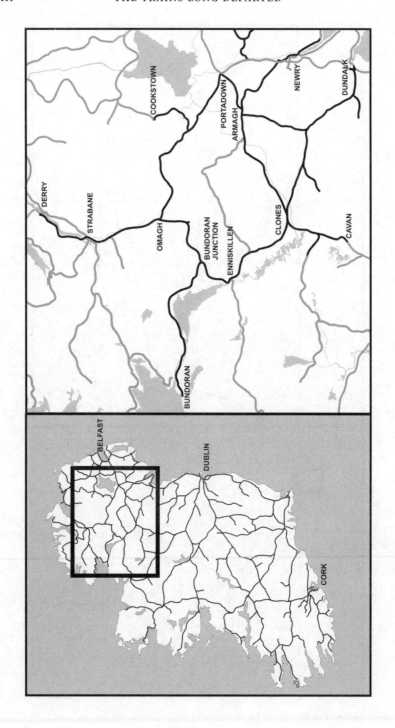

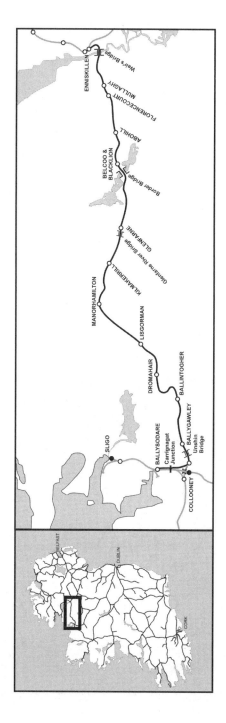

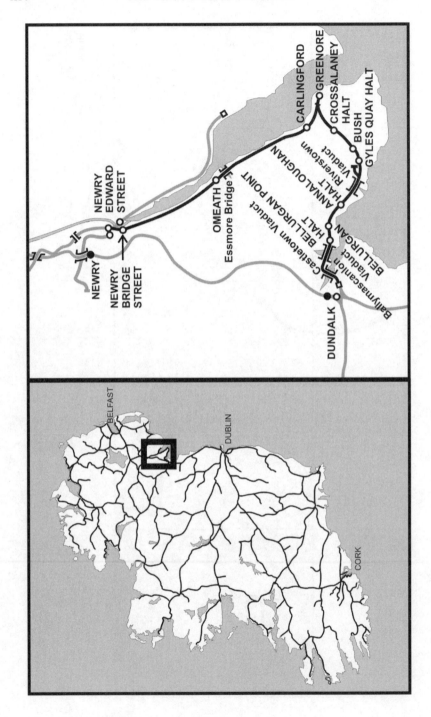

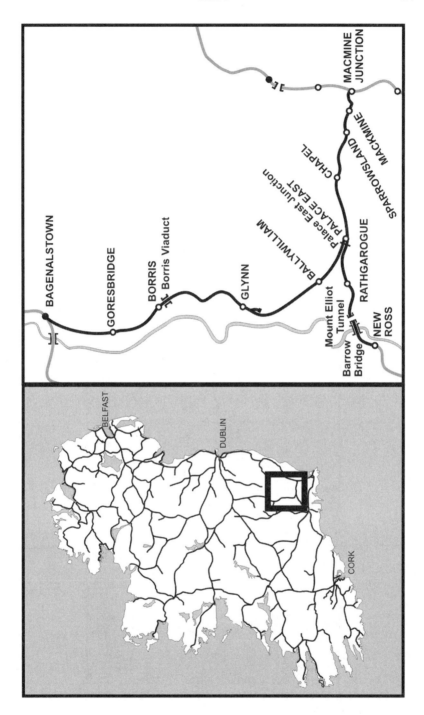

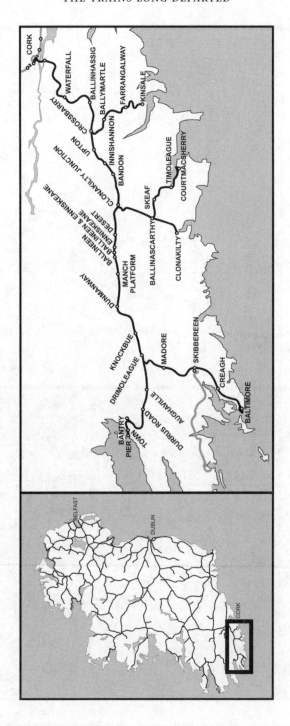

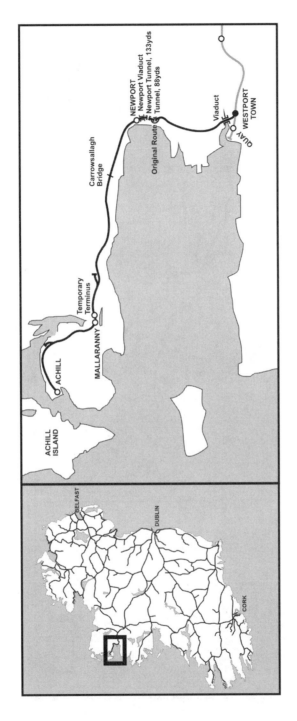

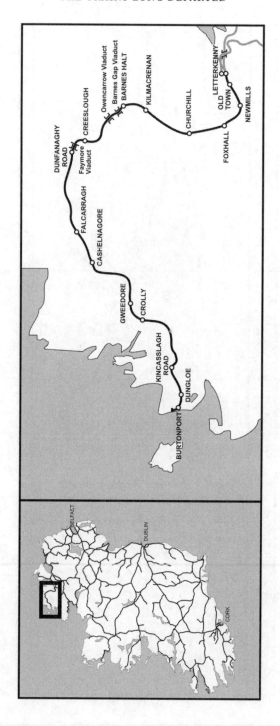

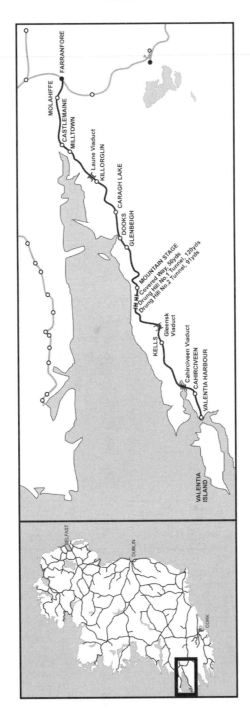

INTRODUCTION

The first railway in Ireland, the short 5½ mile long line between Dublin and Kingstown, was opened to the public on 17 December 1834. It took a while for railway construction to get into its stride after this modest beginning. It was to be 1839 before the next line opened—the first section of the Ulster Railway from Belfast to Lisburn. There had been a false start in the meantime with the so-called 'railway mania' of the 1830s when numerous schemes were proposed, almost all of which floundered in the worsening economic conditions towards the end of that decade. Another brake on development at this time was the decision of the government to become involved in the planning of a network of railways for the country. A Royal Commission was announced in March 1836 whose purpose was to recommend an appropriate national railway network for Ireland. One of the reasons behind the appointment of the Commission was a feeling in government and business circles that, because the Irish economy was so fragile and underdeveloped, the industrial and market forces which were driving railway construction in the rest of the kingdom, and the ability of the capital markets to fund this expensive process, could not be relied upon.

However, as often happens when governments become involved in matters of strategic planning, there was no connection between the aspiration to do something and the provision for the means to achieve this. Because there was no serious suggestion that public money would be provided to build up the network of lines proposed by the Commissioners, their report was shelved and its recommendations were completely ignored, even down to its choice of a gauge for Ireland's railways which only the Ulster Railway, to its cost, adopted.

It was not until the 1840s that railway building began in earnest. By then any thoughts of government involvement had evaporated and the process of railway construction in Ireland was left largely to the private sector for the next forty years. This brings us back to the issue which the setting up of the Commission has acknowledged in the first place, the weakness of the Irish economy and the question as to whether Irish capitalists could raise the huge sums of money required to build miles of railways across the country. By the end of the 1840s, the economic outlook was far worse than it had been in the 1830s as the appalling economic and social consequences of the Great Famine were beginning to become apparent. However, despite that, it was that decade of despair which saw the main arteries of a nationwide network of railways being formed. Dublin was connected to Cork by 1849, the main line of the Midland Great Western system which would eventually link Dublin to Galway and Sligo was begun, and the lines which would connect Dublin with Belfast were partly open by the end of the 1840s. In Ulster, the first sections of what would become the Belfast & County Down and the Belfast & Northern Counties systems were opened.

Cross-country routes were also beginning to take shape. In the north-west, the Londonderry & Enniskillen began services from Derry to Strabane in 1847 and on the east coast the Dundalk & Enniskillen opened its line from Dundalk to Castleblayney in 1849, though more than ten years were to pass before the two concerns would eventually meet at their intended destination in County Fermanagh. Further south, the Waterford & Limerick line had opened to goods and passengers as far as Limerick Junction and Tipperary by May 1848, just before the Great Southern & Western line from Dublin got that far, though it would be 1854 before the W&L could scrape together enough funds to extend its tracks to Waterford.

That this early frenzy of railway construction took place at the very time when Irish society and the Irish economy were being convulsed by the Great Famine made the achievements of these railway pioneers all the more remarkable. These huge engineering projects which were consuming millions of pounds of capital were being driven forward as hundreds of thousands of people were destitute or dying from disease and starvation. There is no doubt that the railway construction projects of the 1840s, some of which received government loans though not outright grants, did provide work for many labourers and a livelihood for their families who would otherwise have been in even more dire straits, but it was hardly an auspicious time to embark on such major enterprises. Indeed it can be argued that the shadow cast over the country for the next century by the legacy of the Great Famine was to play a key role in the history of many of the lines that feature in this book and contributed to their ultimate demise.

The lack of any planned national network meant that railway building was carried on by scores of independent companies who were normally interested only in making a case for their own line and its likely returns without much regard for the national picture. The network of railways across the country was therefore built up in a piecemeal fashion and for the next eight decades construction continued in a series of fits and starts, driven by a variety of motives. Despite this lack of planning, the end result was a genuinely national network which peaked at just under 3,500 route miles at around the time of the Great War. By then, railways served every one of the thirty-two counties, and even allowing for obvious no-go areas for rail tracks by dint of their physical geography—areas such as the Sperrin and Wicklow Mountains, parts of Connemara and north-west Mayo—there were few habitations of any size which were more than twenty miles from one of the country's over 1,400 railway stations.

A comprehensive history of the rise and fall of this once great national asset and the belated recent resurgence of at least parts of it is given in my previous book published by Gill & Macmillan, *Irish Railways, A New History*, and it was the positive response to that book which encouraged my publishers to ask me to return to the subject with the suggestion that this time I should focus on some of the more interesting and significant lines that are no longer with us. I was immediately taken with this idea. The only difficulty was in selecting the lines that should be included out of the huge number that had been closed in the course of the last century. Sadly, I was spoiled for choice. When the railways of England, Scotland and Wales came under wartime government control in 1914 the network amounted to around 20,000 route miles. Given the differences in size and population between the two islands and the absence of significant mineral resources in Ireland, especially coal, which was a huge stimulus to railway development across the Irish Sea, the railway network in Ireland, while much smaller, was of a respectable size. Today, there are about 10,000 route miles in existence on the other island, around half that which existed in 1914. In Ireland the rate of attrition has been much higher, with less than a third of the 1914 route mileage surviving.

All over the country are to be found the decaying remains of railways which were promoted with the greatest of optimism throughout the course of the nineteenth century. While nature has inexorably reclaimed cuttings and embankments, man has been responsible for the demolition of scores of stations, bridges and viaducts. Track and signalling equipment has been dismantled and farmers have taken back land which was wrested from their nineteenth-century forebears by the railway builders. Looking at these remains in the landscape, some of which have now degenerated to such an extent that they are unrecognisable as the trackbeds of former railways unless you knew they were there in the first place, it is hard to believe how quickly they have passed on from their former glory. They have quickly become like Neolithic burial mounds or other archaeological features weakly transmitting faint signals from an ancient culture, no more than hinting at what they were like when they were in their prime. Yet the majority of these abandoned railways were open to serve the public well within living memory, though it is also a salutary thought that some of these lines, such as those from Galway to

Clifden and from Westport to Achill, have now been abandoned for close to twice as long as they were operational.

The railways were abandoned in piecemeal fashion, which resembled the way they had been built in the first place. One result of this was that there was no attempt on either side of the border to retain the formations of abandoned railways for possible future use. However, in the Republic in the case of some of the lines closed after the 1960s, the track was allowed to remain in situ for many years after the last service had run in case a need for the line arose from some circumstance unforeseen when the trains stopped running. This happened in the case of part of the Waterford to Mallow line which closed in 1967. A 26 mile long section from Suir Bridge Junction in Waterford to near Dungarvan was reopened in 1970. Indeed, a 1½ mile section, complete with three new level crossings, was added to the original route to serve a magnesite works at Ballinacourty. The plant and the railway serving it lasted until 1982. In the case of the line from Claremorris to Collooney, which lost its passenger services in 1963 and was closed completely in 1975, most of the track was never lifted and even though substantial trees are growing through the rotting remnants of the sleepers in places, the fact that the railway still just about exists makes the work of those gallant campaigners who are seeking to have it reopened much easier. If nothing remained on the ground and the formation had been sold off piecemeal their already difficult task would be all but impossible.

Admittedly with the benefit of hindsight, it is a great pity that the many miles of abandoned railway lines throughout Ireland could not have been used to create a new national network of footpaths or cycleways. The generally flat formation devoid of steep gradients to which the steam locomotive did not take kindly make abandoned railways ideal for the cyclist who is usually equally averse to steep climbs. Another reason for retaining the trackbeds intact—which again it would be unrealistic to have expected the former operators or their political masters to prophesy—was the renaissance in railways which began to gain momentum, in mainland Europe at least, from the 1970s onwards though its arrival in Ireland was to be much later. No one involved in ripping up all those miles of track, from the 1930s to the 1970s, could ever have conceived that a railway might once again be built on that formation many years in the future.

The first instance of this in Ireland was the revival of part of the former Dublin & South Eastern Railway line from Harcourt Street station in Dublin to Bray as part of the city's splendid Luas tramway system. The Harcourt Street line was one of the most controversial closures of that era in the Republic when it occurred on the last day of 1958. By luck or judgment most of the formation survived after the rails had been lifted, to be brought back to life when the trams began to run in the new millennium. The next completely abandoned route to be resuscitated will be part of the former Midland Great Western line from Clonsilla to Navan which lost its passenger services as long ago as January 1947 and was closed completely by Córas Iompair Éireann in April 1963. Part of this line will again see passenger trains in the autumn of 2010. When these and the many other hundreds of miles of railways were closed the car, the bus and the lorry were king and the railways were largely seen as an anachronism from another age. The radically different economic and demographic circumstances that have driven these reopenings could not have been imagined by even the most optimistic visionary when those lines were originally closed.

As time rolls inexorably on, it is easy to forget the immense effort called for to build even the most modest of branch lines in the nineteenth century. The idea for such a line often sprung up from within the local community. A theme which crops up again and again is the very laudable Victorian aspiration of improvement. In this case it was not the improvement of an individual which provided the motivation but that of the locality and its economic prospects. In a world where the only alternative to the train was the horse, railways were frequently seen as embodying the spirit of the age. The genesis of a line might come out of informal meetings and conversations among groups of landowners or local business people who felt it was imperative to have a railway to serve their town or district lest it was left behind by places already with rail connections. Once a decision was made to go ahead with the line a provisional committee might be formed whose main task was to publish a prospectus for the scheme.

The promoters then had to form a company and begin to negotiate the two major impediments which faced all such schemes, raising the money and obtaining approval from parliament in the form of an Act which allowed them official sanction to negotiate the compulsory purchase of the land required to lay their track. Many schemes fell at this hurdle in the face of objections from competing railway companies, hostile landowners and other vested interests. If a railway bill was contested there could be large legal fees to be paid by the promoters, with no assurance of success, and the legislature, then as now, often proceeded at its own pace. However, without this power to effectively override existing property rights, the railway promoters would have been totally at the mercy of truculent and grasping landowners opposed to the scheme. Even with the Act in their pockets, local bigwigs could still cause railway promoters much grief as happened to those of the Portadown, Dungannon & Omagh Junction Railway who were forced to build a completely unnecessary 814 yards long tunnel to the south of Dungannon at the insistence of the local landowner, Lord Northland, who did not want the view across his parkland spoiled, as he saw it, by the passage of trains.

Once parliamentary approval for a line had been secured, the real problem for many Irish lines came into sharp focus—how to obtain the funds to build it. Railways were capital-intensive beasts then as now. Money had to be raised with only the promise of future dividends as security. The number of schemes that ran into difficulties in raising the capital to build their line would make for a very long list. Sometimes the Commissioners for Public Works would provide loans for schemes which were in trouble, and even though government attitudes to financing railways in Ireland changed towards the end of the nineteenth century, for the great majority of smaller concerns who built their lines before the 1880s funding was invariably a struggle. If money was slow to come in and a line was not built within the time stipulated in the company's Act of Parliament, the powers conferred in that Act would expire and another expensive trip back to Westminster was required to have them renewed.

A decision had to be made at some point whether the local company would work its own line, which meant finding more funds to buy locomotives, carriages and wagons and perhaps to build workshops to maintain them, or whether they should entrust their line's working to one of the larger companies, perhaps the one with which their line made a junction. If they chose the latter option, remuneration to the company entrusted with the working of their line was usually in the form of a hefty percentage of the receipts. In 1861 the Finn Valley Railway made an agreement to pay the Dundalk & Enniskillen, soon to change its name to the Irish North Western Railway, to work their line from Strabane to Stranorlar for 35 per cent of gross receipts. In addition the FVR was charged an annual rental of £375 for the use of the INWR station at Strabane. Faced with a stagnant economy, frequent agricultural depressions and a falling population, it is not surprising that many small railway companies struggled, and the ultimate fate which befell countless local lines in Ireland was that the original proprietors were sooner or later forced to sell out to one of the bigger companies. The Great Southern & Western, by far Ireland's biggest railway company, was notorious for hoovering up smaller companies for a fraction of the cost it had taken to build the lines in the first place.

A new element in the financing of railway building in Ireland came into play from the 1880s onwards. The British government began to at last take some interest in the bleak economic conditions which prevailed in large parts of Ireland. There was an element of political expediency in this. Some historians have referred to this shift in policy as constructive unionism; others of a more cynical disposition have described it as an attempt to kill Home Rule with kindness, though the origin of this description came from one of the policy's advocates (see page 147). Whatever its motivation, in keeping with the generally held view that the spread of railways was a key to economic growth and prosperity, there was a concerted attempt to increase the number of miles of railway in the country. Figures produced by the Board of Trade showed that in 1881 there were 2,441 route miles of railway open throughout Ireland. Given the difficulties in raising capital in an economically backward country, this was quite an impressive outcome from forty years of railway building.

An imprecise comparison with Scotland, where king coal was mined in many places, shows that in the mid-1870s there were about 2,600 miles of railway in use in that part of the kingdom. However, there were still many parts of Ireland, notably in Donegal, Mayo, Cork and Kerry, which were many miles from a railhead. The size of the network in 1881 was probably about as big as conventional methods of railway promotion could deliver. Capitalists clearly needed incentives to encourage them to take the railway into those parts of the country where a reasonable return on their investment was far from likely and it was government-backed inducements which spurred on the last great phase of railway building that occupied the final decades of the nineteenth century.

These incentives came in two forms. Before the County Councils were established in 1898, local government was in the hands of Grand Juries, unelected bodies often dominated by local landowners whose main purpose was to levy local rates from the baronies into which the counties were subdivided. The Tramways Act passed in 1883 allowed the Grand Juries to guarantee the interest on the capital used to build railways which met their approval by imposing what was known as a baronial guarantee on the ratepayers of the districts served by that railway. Interest on capital employed in building these railways was guaranteed at rates of up to 5 per cent. At a stroke, this transformed the building of light railways and tramways in remote parts of Ireland from being a highly risky business to a gilt-edged investment, with the return on the capital employed guaranteed by the unfortunate ratepayers who had little say in the matter.

At first baronial guarantees were applicable only to narrow gauge lines which cost less to build, but later they were made available to broad gauge schemes as well. This measure was followed by two more railway Acts passed at Westminster in 1889 and 1896. The first of these allowed direct government funding for lines which the Lord Lieutenant deemed to be in the public interest. This Act is sometimes called the Balfour Act after the man responsible for it, Arthur Balfour, Chief Secretary for Ireland at the time. The second Act went even further and almost set the government up as a railway promoter as it allowed the Treasury to make grants available to build lines which the government deemed were necessary. Incentives like these were not offered elsewhere in the kingdom and were largely responsible for that last 1,000 miles of railway built between 1880 and 1914.

With this active official encouragement and, it must be said, some protests from the ratepayers (especially after 1898 when they had a vote at last), who were sometimes understandably reluctant to be press-ganged into funding this final phase of railway construction, the national network was eventually completed. Ireland's railways then embarked on their brief age of relative prosperity which can be broadly defined as the years from the 1880s to 1914 when they had a virtual monopoly of the traffic on offer. Even if this was modest, at least receipts normally outweighed working expenses in this period. This impression of success was actually illusory because those lines on the margins, notably most of the narrow gauge schemes encouraged by the Tramways Act of 1883, could never generate anything like enough profit to allow them to invest in their track and equipment. This meant that often such lines had to continue to use the locomotives and rolling stock which had been supplied for their opening throughout their entire existence, running on increasingly battered track which again they could not afford to renew. As the twentieth century wore on lines such as the Clogher Valley Railway which ran through Tyrone and Fermanagh and the Cavan & Leitrim and Tralee & Dingle sections of the Great Southern Railways became great value for the railway enthusiast but hard work for those who had to run them or who depended on their services.

By the end of the nineteenth century there had been a considerable amount of consolidation in terms of ownership, with perhaps over 75 per cent of the route miles in the hands of the larger companies. Ulster was dominated by the Great Northern and the Belfast & Northern Counties companies while the Belfast & County Down, scarcely a large operation with only 80 route miles, held sway in most of that hilly northern county. Further south, the major players included the Midland Great Western with its main lines from Dublin to Galway and Sligo and the Dublin & South Eastern, like the B&CDR, another compact system stretching down the east coast from Dublin to Wexford and across to Waterford. The Cork, Bandon & South Coast Railway held sway in the west of County Cork and the main routes of the Waterford, Limerick & Western straggled down the west coast from Sligo to Limerick, across to Waterford and through north Kerry to Tralee. However, all of these were eclipsed by the Great Southern & Western, the country's largest railway, which at the height of its pomp operated over 1,000 route miles of track, about one third of the entire national network. This included the erstwhile WL&W, which amalgamated with the GS&WR in 1901.

From a position of relative security, for many of the lines built with such effort and optimism in the previous century, the going suddenly got a whole lot tougher in the second decade of the new century. The first assault on the railways came about as a consequence of a political landscape which had changed radically since 1914. The treaty of 1921 which had ended the War of

Independence resulted in an international border stretching across the north of the country, cutting across time-honoured trading routes and patterns, many of which the railways had been built to exploit. An oft-quoted statistic is that the lines of the GNR crossed the new border at seventeen different locations. The location of the border was defined by a crude sectarian head-count across the counties concerned, yet this soon began to affect economic activity as differing tariff regimes began to be put in place where previously trade and goods had moved freely. This created some Gilbertian anomalies. The Sligo, Leitrim & Northern Counties Railway station built to serve the two small contiguous villages of Belcoo and Blacklion was now dealing with goods and passengers from two different states. The border placed Belcoo in County Fermanagh in Northern Ireland, whilst Blacklion in County Cavan was in the Free State. Not far from Belcoo & Blacklion station was Pettigo on the GNR branch to Bundoran. Here the village's station was in the Irish Free State whereas most of the village itself was in Northern Ireland.

Where trains crossed the border, journeys took longer as services had to stop at two sets of Customs posts established at the stations closest to the border. Passengers were delayed and harassed as their luggage was examined, but more importantly goods and livestock were held up at the border as the new bureaucrats ensured that all the correct forms were filled in and any duty owing was paid. To avoid this nonsense, there was suddenly an incentive for business people in border towns such as Monaghan to deal with firms in Dublin rather than Belfast as they would have been doing since the Ulster Railway's line had reached their town in 1858.

While the northern railway companies had to deal with problems posed by the new border, in what was now the Irish Free State civil war broke out between pro- and anti-treaty forces. The railway infrastructure had escaped with relatively little damage between 1916 and 1921, but now the anti-treaty Irregulars embarked on an orgy of destruction to deny the use of the railways to Free State forces. Trains were deliberately wrecked and stations and signal cabins were blown up or burnt. One of the most spectacular outrages occurred on the night of 10 January 1923 when the very substantial terminus at Sligo was reduced to smoking rubble with explosives and incendiaries, though perhaps the most disruptive acts of sabotage in this period were the destruction of Ballyvoile viaduct on the Mallow to Waterford line and the Blackwater viaduct just south of Mallow which cut the main Dublin to Cork line. The latter was attacked in August 1922 though a new bridge was built commendably quickly and the line reopened in October 1923.

This disruption would have been bad enough in itself, but it occurred at a time when an even bigger long-term threat to the railways was starting to flex its muscles. The war that had raged across Europe from 1914 to 1918 was characterised by huge advances in technologies of all kinds. Mostly this was focused on finding more efficient ways of killing people be it with poison gas, ever more destructive explosives or by improving the designs of submarines or aircraft. However, one technology which came of age in the midst of all the carnage was the internal combustion engine. As early as 1914, the British Army requisitioned hundreds of London buses to use as troop carriers in France and this set the pattern for a huge growth in the number of internal combustion powered vehicles which carried on throughout the war. From being a novelty in 1914, by the end of the war petrol-engined buses, lorries and cars of all types were much more common. There was also a large number of ex-army vehicles available at cheap prices at the conclusion of hostilities and enterprising individuals, many of them ex-army men who had learned to drive in the course of their service, began to operate these vehicles in a totally unregulated market competing directly with the railways. Eventually, both north and south of the border, regulations governing the use of privately owned buses and lorries were put in place, but there could be no going back to the status quo ante bellum and the already fragile finances of many Irish railways would be fatally challenged by competition from this cheaper and much more flexible mode of transportation in the years ahead.

In 1925 the Irish Free State tackled the parlous finances and damaged infrastructure of its railway companies by sponsoring the amalgamation of the previously independent companies to form one large one, the Great Southern Railways. The new company embraced almost all the lines that operated solely within the twenty-six counties, though a few exceptions such as the astonishing Lartigue monorail which ran from Listowel to Ballybunion in County Kerry were left out in the cold and closed shortly afterwards. This strict policy created its own anomalies. Both of the big narrow gauge operators in County Donegal—the Londonderry & Lough Swilly and the County Donegal Railways—were not included in the GSR because their tracks entered Northern Ireland. In the case of the L&LSR less than five of its 99 miles were in Northern Ireland. This was also the reason that the Sligo, Leitrim & Northern Counties retained its independence even though close to three-quarters of its route mileage lay in the Free State. In Northern Ireland there was no amalgamation or reorganisation; the companies carried on as before, though this lack of a patron made the small ones very vulnerable.

The inter-war years were grim ones on both sides of the border. With the overall population still in its post-Famine decline, there was little prosperity anywhere and the international trade depression which followed from the Wall Street Crash of 1929 ratcheted up the misery. To make matters worse in the south, in 1932 the Fianna Fáil government of Éamon de Valera withheld the payment of land annuities due to the British government and this led to the country being embroiled in the so-call Economic War. When it came to inflicting pain on each other through punitive tariffs, there could only be one winner and the economy of the Free State was not it. It was against this background that the first railway closures began, the start of a melancholy process which was to continue for the next forty years. In Northern Ireland, the roots of a policy of indifference to the railways at best or hostility at worst can also be traced back to the 1930s. The government sponsored the creation of the Northern Ireland Road Transport Board to take over the activities of private bus and lorry operators in the province but at the cost of prohibiting the railway companies from operating bus or lorry feeder services themselves. The Board, which was supposed to co-ordinate the activities of road and rail transport in Northern Ireland, became in effect a government-backed competitor to the railways.

There was a brief resurgence for the railways of both parts of Ireland during World War Two when private motoring was all but abolished because of fuel shortages. In Northern Ireland, which had an important strategic role in the war both as a base for Allied operations during the Battle of the Atlantic and later as a training camp for thousands of American soldiers preparing for D-Day, the railways were busier than they had been for decades. The Irish Free State was neutral during the conflict, and by 1940 rail services began to be badly affected by a shortage of the British coal on which the railways had always depended. At a time when the demand for rail transport was greater than it had been for years, only very limited goods and passenger services could be provided. Towards the latter part of the war, worsening coal shortages led to the drastic reduction of services even on the main lines in the Free State and the temporary closure of many branch lines. While the railways in both jurisdictions were making substantial profits during the wartime restrictions on motoring, as supplies of oil began to return to normal the financial position of the railways deteriorated and losses again became the order of the day.

By 1950 most of Ireland's railways were in public ownership. CIÉ, formed to replace the GSR and run the whole of the Free State's public transport services in 1945, was fully nationalised in 1950. In the north, the Ulster Transport Authority was established in 1948 to take over the operations of the NIRTB and the lines run by the Northern Counties Committee. In 1903, the English Midland Railway had bought the B&NCR. The Midland then became part of the London, Midland & Scottish Railway when Britain's railways were amalgamated into four large, GSR-style companies in 1923. When these companies were nationalised by the British government in 1948, the LMS lines in Northern Ireland were bought by the UTA along with those operated by the B&CDR. Only the GNR and the SL&NCR retained their independence, but by 1950 the wartime prosperity of the GNR had evaporated and as the company ran out of money to continue its operations in the face of growing losses, both governments effectively nationalised it, setting up the Great Northern Railway Board to run its affairs.

These post-war years were bleak ones for the railways of Ireland in which huge chunks of the national network which had taken so long to create were closed down. Both governments were seduced by a misguided policy which deluded them that the railways could once again be brought back into profit. All you had to do was close down a bit more of the network and you were nearly there. When the balance sheet still remained inexplicably in the red, those at the top table would close a few more lines and so it went on. One aspect often overlooked in this process which led to the piecemeal closure of branch lines and secondary routes was their value in feeding traffic on to the remaining main lines. There is no sense of strategy in any of this; it was short termism of the worst kind. While many lines in what was now the Irish Republic either lost their passenger services or were closed completely, policy towards the railways south of the border was almost benign compared to the wholesale destruction which was wrought on the railways in Northern Ireland.

By the time the UTA was finally abolished in 1967, there were only about 200 route miles left open in Northern Ireland and there was a gaping, ugly hole in the railway map of Ireland. The UTA and their political masters at Stormont were the guilty parties. Soon after its takeover, most of the former NCC routes, apart from the lines from Belfast to Londonderry, Portrush and Larne, were closed. The same fate befell the B&CDR, with only the branch to Bangor being retained. The closure of the GNR lines from Dundalk to Enniskillen, Omagh, Cavan and Bundoran in 1957, which in turn led to the closure of the SL&NCR—as there was no outlet for its traffic beyond Enniskillen—and the line from Portadown to Derry in 1965, meant that there were no railways at all left in the counties of Donegal, Tyrone, Fermanagh and Monaghan. The only rails left in County Armagh were the few miles of the Dublin to Belfast line which passed through parts of the county. The last section of the goods-only CIÉ line to Kingscourt was the one remaining stretch of railway left in County Cavan. In addition, railway goods services within Northern Ireland ended in 1965. The consequence of this madness is that there is now a huge area— it must be close to one third of the land mass of the island—which does not have access to a railway. In the space of a few years, for reasons we will try to fathom elsewhere, the UTA managed to destroy not just the railways serving the areas listed above but the very concept of a national network which had taken so long to put in place. With no railways operating in such a large part of the country, we can no longer say that Ireland has a truly nationwide network of railways.

While politicians in the Republic pursued the same misguided chimera that drove the UTA and the Stormont government to close down most of the lines in Ulster in their futile search for a profitable railway, this madness took on a thankfully less aggressive form south of the border. Having stated that, many hundreds of miles of track were closed in the Republic from the 1950s through to the 1970s. The difference was that what remained did more or less serve most of the state. The only counties in the Republic which do not have a single railway station offering passenger services are Donegal, Monaghan and Cavan, and as we have seen, the blame for that lay elsewhere. By the 1980s all the remaining lines radiated out from Dublin, with one exception, that from Limerick to Rosslare. Apart from that, all the other secondary routes such as those from Limerick to Tralee and Sligo and from Mallow to Waterford, and any remaining branch lines, had been closed.

If you drew a graph showing the growth of the Irish railway network and its subsequent decline, both sides would look almost identical. It took about the same amount of time for the network to reach its peak as it did to plunge to its nadir, and the spike of openings in the 1840s and 1850s would be matched on the other side of the graph by a similar spike of closures between 1955 and 1975.

This book is not intended to be a definitive history of the lines which have closed or a forensic investigation of all the reasons for their closure. Rather it is a reflection on the history of just a few of the lines that have gone and an attempt to recall something of their unique character. Some may feel that lines other than those selected merit inclusion and they are probably right to do so as no two railways were the same.

Railways are complex organic creatures, amounting to much more than the sum of their individual components, and they depended on the diverse skills of all the people who worked on them. The footplate crews could go nowhere without the co-operation of the signalmen or the work of the men responsible for keeping the track in a safe condition. When a line was closed this close-knit team was also disbanded and their skills were lost forever. Every line had its own personality and its own stories. In truth, many of the lines which have closed did outlive their usefulness but hundreds of miles of track across the length and breadth of Ireland were ripped up for no good reason, and as the planet begins to get warmer and the unrestricted use of the car becomes less tenable, we may live to regret the loss of so many lines which could well be providing a valuable public service to this day.

What follows in these pages is a celebration of some of those lines from which the trains have long departed, for good, and a few observations on what remains to be seen of them today. The lines selected are ones that have seized my imagination in the course of many years of researching the history of Ireland's railways. The great majority of the routes featured in this book were closed before I was old enough to be let out on my own or could afford the price of a ticket to travel on them, so I have been trying to recreate for my own pleasure and I hope for those who sit down with this book, journeys which you and I will never be able to make. Revisiting some of the places they served has been a delight and sometimes it is only when you retrace the routes the tracks followed on the ground that you can fully appreciate the genius or the folly that led to their conception. This virtual railtour will take us from the shores of Red Bay in County Antrim to the end of the pier at Baltimore in County Cork and to many places in between. The starting signal has dropped, the engine has whistled, we're away.

Chapter 1 ∿

FROM IRON ORE TO CHARABANCS: THE BALLYMENA, CUSHENDALL & RED BAY RAILWAY

A
s far as I can determine, there were no other railway companies in Ireland and few anywhere else in the world that manifestly failed to serve the places mentioned in their titles. The subject of this chapter is a member of that exclusive and slightly oddball club. The Ballymena, Cushendall & Red Bay Railway certainly started out from Ballymena but given the course it followed, from a geographical perspective, it would have been virtually impossible for it to have reached either the village of Cushendall or anywhere else on the shores of Red Bay in County Antrim. From its eventual terminus, at a remote spot called Retreat Castle, over 1,000 ft above sea level in the shadow of the lofty peak of Crockalough, it was possible to look down on the village of Cushendall several miles distant at the foot of Glen Ballyemon, though most of the great vista of Red Bay would have been obscured by Crockalough and the neighbouring peak of Lurigethan or Lurigathan as it was spelt in early twentieth-century Ordnance Survey maps. The correct spelling of Irish place names, if there is such a thing in the case of names transcribed phonetically by the first surveyors from the Gaelic, is often very hard to determine. However, given the reasons for the building of the line in the first place, its failure to reach the

locations mentioned in its title was not important. The BC&RB was that rarity in Ireland, a line driven by the imperative to transport the mineral resources of the area it served which in this instance was principally iron ore.

The easy availability of coal and iron was the foundation on which the Industrial Revolution across the Irish Sea was built. The acknowledged birthplace of the Industrial Revolution, the Ironbridge Gorge in Shropshire, had coal and iron deposits in the vicinity, but as the demands of industry expanded the net had to be cast wider to feed the insatiable demand of the furnaces for the raw materials needed for the production of iron and steel. As an indication of just how voracious was industry's appetite for iron ore in its various forms, between 1850 and 1885 production in Scotland alone averaged about two million tons per year. One area where such heavy industry was thriving was in what is now Cumbria in the north-west of England. The original local sources of ore in locations such as Egremont and Cleator Moor, which had encouraged the iron industry to take root there in the first place, began to run into geological difficulties and the ironmasters had to look elsewhere for their supplies of ore. Fortunately, there was a potentially useful source of iron ore not far away across the Irish Sea in County Antrim. Those building blocks of the Industrial Revolution, coal and iron ore, were found there. In different circumstances, they might have amounted to something. The small-scale mining of coal and iron had been taking place, certainly around Ballycastle on the north coast of Antrim, since the seventeenth century and this activity gave rise to some of the first recorded railroads or tramways in Ireland which were operating there in the mid-eighteenth century.

In the middle of the nineteenth century, the scale of iron ore mining in north-east Antrim began to increase as a ready market for the ore produced was found across the Irish Sea. At first the ore was taken by carts down to the coast to locations like the pier at the north end of Red Bay from where it was loaded on to ships for the journey to the furnaces of Scotland and the north-west of

England. Those carters must have been tough individuals working in often inhospitable conditions on roads which left much to be desired. In 1872, just before the coming of the railway, an aerial ropeway to carry minerals was built from Cargan to the pier at Red Bay. The ropeway was apparently sabotaged by the carters who saw it as a threat to their livelihood. They would have found the railway a much tougher proposition. The poor transport links in the area were an impediment to the mining industry. Those piers and harbours which did exist, such as the one at Red Bay, could only accommodate small vessels and were prone to silting up.

Getting Antrim ore to market was a problem for which a railway was seen as the answer. The BC&RB was authorised by parliament in July 1872, its Act permitting the railway to be built to a gauge of between 2 and 3 ft. It was only the second narrow gauge railway to be authorised in Ireland. The first, the Ennis & West Clare Railway, which got its Act the previous year was never built. However, it was not the first narrow gauge line to be opened in Ireland. This distinction fell to another line located a short distance away from the BC&RB's eventual terminus, a railway also built to exploit the mineral wealth of the Antrim glens but one which was destined to be very short lived and spectacularly unsuccessful.

The activities of the Glenariff Iron Ore & Harbour Company were based entirely on lands owned by the Earl of Antrim. Because the company did not need to infringe the property rights of anyone else other than those of his lordship whose co-operation they already had, no Act of Parliament was required to build their railway which was 4½ miles long and ran from mines and adits at Cloughcor near the head of Glenariff to a new pier at Milltown. The Earl of Antrim was rewarded with a royalty of one shilling/five pence on every ton of ore extracted. The railway crossed the Antrim Coast Road on the White Arch near Waterfoot, the remains of which stand to this day. A few blocks of stone can still be seen in the water alongside the road just south of the White Arch, useful resting places for sea birds, all that remain of the pier which could accommodate vessels of up to 2,000 tons built to be served by the railway. The pier was destroyed in a storm in November 1898, long after the railway had been abandoned. Houses were built near Milltown for the miners who probably hitched a ride to the mines at the top of the glen on the trains though officially no passenger services ever ran on the line. From the White Arch, the trackbed can still be traced running up the south-west side of the glen, steadily climbing from the floor of the valley. Two miles from the coast at Greenaghan, there was a substantial viaduct which carried the line 70 ft over Altmore Burn. The company owned at least five or six steam locomotives, two of which were eventually sold to the Londonderry & Lough Swilly Railway when the L&LSR converted its existing line to the 3 ft gauge in 1885 (see Chapter 8). This was a proper railway solidly built, not a tramway, but it was soon in difficulties for geological reasons. The line was only in regular use from 1873 until 1876 when the seams of high quality ores which the original surveys had identified began to run out. The railway was finally abandoned in 1885, with its track, remaining rolling stock and other assets sold off in 1888 at the behest of the Earl of Antrim. However, it is the historical significance of the Glenariff line as the pioneer of the 3 ft gauge in Ireland that far outweighs its short and ultimately unsuccessful existence.

With the Glenariff line already up and running, if only for a short time, construction of the BC&RB began. The first 11 miles from Ballymena to Cargan opened in May 1875. A further 2-mile section from Cargan to Parkmore was ready by January 1876, with the final stretch to Retreat open by August of that year. The line was used for goods traffic only, and between Parkmore and Retreat at a place called Essathohan siding it reached the highest point on any Irish railway at 1,045 ft above sea level. From Rathkenny, 6 miles from Ballymena all the way up to Retreat, sidings, tramways and a rope-worked incline fed mineral traffic on to the railway. The wet and windswept Antrim uplands must have been a veritable hive of activity in these early years of the railway as mineral traffic poured on to the line. The Belfast & Northern Counties Railway whose facilities the narrow gauge company shared at Ballymena subscribed over £25,000 of the £90,000 cost of the Red Bay line. The mineral traffic was transferred to broad gauge wagons at Ballymena for onward transit to Belfast and ultimately across the Irish Sea.

At first the tonnages carried were very impressive. In 1880, the year the iron ore traffic was at its peak, over 135,000 tons of ore were conveyed over the B&NCR line to Belfast, most of which would have come down on the narrow gauge from high in the glens. Fortunately the loaded ore trains were assisted by gravity on their way to Ballymena. It was a very sharply graded line and climbed steeply from Rathkenny to the summit at Essathohan siding on gradients as severe as 1 in 40. Once the line was open, there was never any serious attempt to reach the coast at Cushendall or Red Bay. The terminus at Retreat was over 1,000 ft above sea level and that precluded the use of a conventional railway which could not have made such a precipitous descent in the space of four or five miles.

The good times for the BC&RB were short lived. Even though another 3 ft gauge line, the Ballymena & Larne, opened in 1880 and made an end-on junction with it at Ballymena the following year, allowing ore to be shipped directly in 3 ft gauge trucks to the port of Larne without the need to transfer it onto broad gauge wagons, one of the periodic trade depressions which marked the nineteenth century as much as they did the twentieth reduced the demand for iron ore in the mid-1880s. When economic conditions improved cheaper and richer ores were being imported into England, Scotland and Wales from Spain and the trade in ore from County Antrim never recovered to its former level. Faced with declining revenues, in July 1884 the BC&RB was taken over by its neighbour at Ballymena, the B&NCR, after less than ten years of independence, though this was far from the end of its story.

The original line had never carried passengers but the new owners, the B&NCR, obtained permission from the Board of Trade to do this and in April 1886 began to operate passenger services from Ballymena to Knockanally, which was renamed Martinstown in 1920. In 1888 passenger trains were extended to Parkmore 13½ miles from Ballymena though they never ran over the final section of the line from Parkmore to Retreat. Faced with declining mineral traffic and a line serving a thinly populated and remote district, the B&NCR displayed a remarkable degree of enterprise and lateral thinking. The company proceeded to turn the line into a gateway to a tourist attraction of its own creation in an attempt to stimulate both traffic and its revenues.

Not far away from Parkmore station, incidentally the highest in Ireland, was Glenariff. With the abandonment of the mines there, this picturesque glen reverted to being an attraction for visitors. Glenariff was described by the Victorian novelist William Makepeace Thackeray in *The Irish Sketchbook*, published in 1843, as like Switzerland in miniature. The B&NCR leased the glen and in the person of their talented and inventive civil engineer, Berkeley Deane Wise, got to work on it. While most railway civil engineers were concerned with the state of the track, bridges and other structures on which the trains run, this remarkable man set about embellishing the B&NCR and the area it served in the most singular way. He started work for the company in 1888 and in the 18 years up to his retirement on the grounds of failing health in 1906 he rebuilt many stations, often in a mock Tudor style. The Northern Ireland Railways terminus at Portrush and the stations at Antrim and Carrickfergus are other fine examples of his work. Wise was also an early enthusiast for the use of reinforced concrete as a building material. On the B&NCR he used it in a multiplicity of applications, building bridges, signal boxes, sheds, level crossing keepers' houses and even signal posts with this material. Some of these hardy relics of Wise and his passion for concrete can still be seen on former B&NCR lines across Ulster. The B&NCR also did much to stimulate the tourist industry in the parts of the province it served. It opened hotels in Larne and Portrush, and Wise built a magnificent coastal path around the great basalt cliffs near Whitehead known as The Gobbins, with tunnels through the cliffs and spectacular bridges out over the sea. After this opened in 1902, it was claimed, probably by the railway company, to be one of the most popular tourist attractions in Ireland, with more visitors than the Giant's Causeway.

Back at Glenariff, Wise laid out a series of paths and rustic bridges through the glen, snaking over the streams that gushed through it and beside its spectacular waterfalls. Shelters were built at strategic locations so that visitors could sit down and enjoy the views. Then as now the mandatory tea room was required and this was added in 1891. For a time there was a dark room for use by intrepid Victorian and Edwardian photographers whose heavy wooden glass plate cameras were a far cry from those available to us in the digital age. The purpose of all of this was to create an attraction to lure visitors on to the former BC&RB railway. In summer, horse-drawn carriages would meet the trains at Parkmore station to bring visitors to the glen. Those holding rail tickets were allowed in for free; others had to pay an admission charge. Later, tours by horse-drawn carriages and charabancs were organised from Parkmore along parts of the spectacular and nearby Antrim Coast Road which ran along the shore at the foot of Glenariff.

The passenger service provided by the B&NCR between Ballymena and Parkmore was typical of that on so many minor Irish lines. In August 1900, at the peak of the tourist season, there were four trains each way daily but they ran on weekdays only in deference to the Sabbatarian reticence of the owner of the glen who leased it to the railway company. He apparently only relented and allowed it to be opened to the public on Sundays from 1910 onwards. Sunday trains did not run until then. Trains up the hill towards Parkmore took between 47 and 50 minutes. Those freewheeling down the grade were not much quicker though one virtual flyer, the 3.45pm, managed the 13½ miles in 40 minutes. This train provided a five-minute connection at Ballymena into the 2.50pm express from Londonderry to Belfast which would have whisked passengers back to the city by 5.40pm, in nice time for any tourists to have tea in their hotels. In 1903 the line had its second change of ownership when the B&NCR was taken over by the English Midland Railway. The MR lines in Ulster were managed from Belfast through an organisation called the Northern Counties Committee which included local managers and representatives from the MR head office in Derby, but the practical effects of the takeover at track level so to speak were negligible—the same little engines still had to work hard every day as they pounded up the gradients to Cargan and Parkmore.

The two decades before 1914 were the golden years for most Irish railway companies and the closest many of them ever came to prosperity. The Ballymena to Parkmore line was not an exception to this trend. Some ore was still carried though nothing like as much as in the early years of the line's existence. In addition, it provided for the modest transport needs of the small villages it served, carrying local passengers and goods throughout the year. The railway also continued to bring tourists and day trippers to enjoy the delights of Glenariff throughout the summer season. Passenger numbers peaked in the years before the Great War. Out of that shattering conflict staggered a changed world where the internal combustion engine began to emerge as a serious and unregulated competitor to the steam railway. Ireland's own political troubles affected the line in March 1921 when the stations at Cross Roads, Cargan, Parkmore and Retreat were maliciously destroyed by fire. This gallant attempt to resolve the country's complex political and ethnic problems by burning down stations on a remote narrow gauge railway seems inexplicably to have been unsuccessful.

A third change of ownership came about in 1923 when the railway companies in Britain were merged into four large groups. The Midland Railway now became part of the London, Midland

& Scottish Railway which was probably the biggest railway company in the world at that time. Throughout the 1920s in a pattern repeated all over Ireland, and one which seems to have particularly affected the narrow gauge lines, passenger numbers began to tail off. As late as 1929 no fewer than 40,000 people paid six pence each to visit Glenariff though many of these were now probably arriving in cars and on NCC buses. Passenger trains finally ceased to run from 1 October 1930. Goods services along the full length of the line continued until April 1937 when the section from Rathkenny to Retreat closed completely, though goods trains continued to run from Ballymena to serve a creamery at Rathkenny until June 1940.

Quite a few relics of the line have survived into the new millennium. Beyond Cargan, the course of the abandoned railway trackbed is close to the A43 Ballymena to Cushendall road which runs parallel to the old railway for much of the way. Bridges, cuttings and embankments can all be seen. The most remarkable survivor is the former station at Parkmore. This is hidden behind a stand of trees close to the junction of the A43 with the B14. The original station was of largely wooden construction, but after its destruction in 1921 the NCC rebuilt Parkmore in its beloved concrete. It survives remarkably intact, eighty years after it saw its last passenger train. Even the name of the station, embossed in concrete, can be seen and the original water tank on its brick-built plinth is extant. The water tank has plaques at both ends bearing the name of its maker, James Moore & Sons Ltd Engineers Belfast. Beyond Parkmore the line is close to the B14 but much of the trackbed has been lost to the forests planted since it closed. The remains of the stone arched bridge which took the railway over a burn close to the highest point on the Irish railway network still exists parallel to the road. A few miles further on, a ruined grey building standing alone in a field marks the terminus of the line at Retreat.

The fading remains of the railway are in marked contrast to the renaissance which has occurred at Glenariff. The glen was rented from its owners by the railway company until the NCC bought it outright in 1930, ironically the year the passenger service on the railway ended. It was closed during the Second World War but reopened to visitors afterwards. The glen then passed to the Ulster Transport Authority when that state-owned company took over the running of the former LMS lines in Ulster in 1948. Later, the glen and the surrounding estate were acquired by what is now the Forest Service of Northern Ireland and the present forest park opened to the public in 1977. The new owners restored the original paths and bridges to their former glory and once again the trails and waterfalls in this most picturesque of locations are attracting many thousands of visitors every year. I hope a few of those visiting the glen take a moment to reflect on its history and on the industrial heritage of the area where iron and other minerals, including bauxite, were once mined. Every time I travel up towards Parkmore and look down on the long-abandoned trackbed of the railway, I try to picture one of the line's gallant little tank engines grappling with the gradient, perhaps sending up a volcano of smoke as it momentarily lost its grip on a bit of slippery rail, hauling empty wagons to be loaded with iron ore or followed by a short tail of passenger carriages bringing a new batch of excited tourists to enjoy the natural wonders of this most agreeable part of the island.

Chapter 2

GONE NEVER TO RETURN: A LAMENT FOR THE IRISH NORTH AND THE DERRY ROAD

If one has an idle moment, it is quite instructive to take a glance at one of the very good railway maps of western Europe which are available both in print and online. What is striking about these maps is that in most countries the areas which do not have access to a railway are relatively small. There are clearly places where geography dictates that railways will not be found, the mountainous spine of Italy being one obvious example. However, even in the case of Britain, which has had more than its fair share of line closures over the years, a glance at the map will show that it still retains what can clearly be discerned as a national network reaching into most parts of the landmass of the island including its Celtic fringes. The same sadly cannot be said for Ireland and the reason for this is the huge void in the northern part of the island which lost its railways in the 1950s and 1960s. Irrespective of whatever local hardships these closures caused, and there were many, it is the strategic loss of railways in that broad sweep of territory framed by the Dublin to Sligo line in the south, the Belfast to Dublin line in the east and the Belfast to Londonderry route in the north that has deprived Ireland of a truly national railway network, something which our neighbours in mainland Europe take for granted. How the two most important lines that once filled that gap came to be built and how they were lost is the subject of this chapter. The railways concerned are the Great Northern route from Portadown to Derry, always known to Great Northern men as the Derry Road, and the lines from Dundalk to Enniskillen, Bundoran and Omagh. These were referred to by the same GNR men as the Irish North, a nod of the cap to the memory of the company which operated these routes before the formation of the GNR, the Irish North Western Railway.

Two of the companies that built the lines we are discussing were quick out of the blocks when the Railway Mania of the 1840s began. This was the term applied to the spectacular increase in the value of railway shares which occurred in Britain in the middle of that decade as the result of frenzied stock market speculation. Hundreds of railway schemes were floated and money poured into them. As with nearly all sudden stock market booms this was rapidly followed by the bust when the inflated values of railway shares tumbled the following year, leaving many unwise investors ruined. The speculation extended to Ireland and some of the country's major trunk lines were launched on the back of this sudden upturn in the market. This was actually the second Railway Mania as something very similar on a smaller scale had taken place in the mid-1830s and the first of our companies, the Londonderry & Enniskillen, had originally been promoted at that time. The route for the line via Strabane and Omagh was surveyed in 1837 by one of the most eminent engineers of those pioneering years of railway history, George Stephenson, famed for his work on two of Britain's most important early railways, the Stockton & Darlington and the Liverpool & Manchester.

With the collapse in the market in the late 1830s the L&E went into a sort of corporate hibernation before any construction work could take place. The company was resuscitated following a meeting held in Derry in June 1844, and with the revival of the market in railway shares, this time the navvies did get their shovels dirty. The first part of the line from Derry to Strabane opened in 1847. The route was resurveyed in 1845 by another of the great names of the early Victorian railway world in the person of Robert Stephenson, the son of George Stephenson who had been there in the previous decade. Robert was the designer of the famous *Rocket* locomotive which triumphed at the Rainhill locomotive trials held near Liverpool in 1830 to find the most effective type of engine for what was the world's first inter-city railway, the Liverpool & Manchester. *Rocket*'s multi-tubed boiler, through which heat from the fire was drawn by the blast from the chimney, formed the basic template for the hundreds of thousands of steam locomotives used on railways around the world from that time to the present day.

The Belfast newspaper, *The Northern Whig*, noted in October 1844 its 'mingled delight and anxiety at the torrent of speculation and enterprise which has been rushing forward'. It went on to warn about the danger of a slump as had happened in 1838 which would leave the value of shares in uncompleted lines worthless, but such wise counsels were largely ignored as the speculation roared on. The paper may have had in mind the two recently announced separate schemes to link Enniskillen to Dundalk and Newry. The first of these, the Newry & Enniskillen, was one of the least competent and successful companies which ever managed to run a train service in Ireland. In the light of subsequent events a prediction made by those promoting the N&E, which was published in the *Northern Whig* in October 1844, anticipating dividends of 15 per cent for those who invested in the company, was clearly close to being on the fraudulent side of optimistic.

It took the company eight years to raise enough money to build the first part of its route, the four miles from Newry to a junction with the Dublin to Belfast line at Goraghwood. By the time that great feat had been achieved the authority given in its Act of Parliament to build the rest of the line to Enniskillen had expired. Thwarted in its efforts to get to Enniskillen, in 1857 the company changed its name to the Newry & Armagh and then took another seven years to construct the 18 mile long line to Armagh which occasioned the construction of the longest railway tunnel in Ireland, the 1,759 yards long Lisummon tunnel. Never successful and fated to be the line on which Ireland's most terrible railway smash, the Armagh disaster, occurred in 1889, when it finally closed completely in 1955 an original use was at least found for part of Lisummon tunnel—the growing of mushrooms.

The floundering progress of the Newry & Enniskillen left the field open for the other company with its eyes set on the County Fermanagh town, the Dundalk & Enniskillen. The first section of its route from Dundalk to Castleblayney was opened on 15 February 1849, the same day as the first part of the Dublin & Belfast Junction Railway's line from Drogheda to Portadown which was to become a component of the through route between Belfast and Dublin. In 1849, D&BJR trains started from Newfoundwell, a temporary station just north of Drogheda as the great viaduct which would carry the line over the River Boyne had not yet been built. The D&E line began from a station at Barrack Street in the town and as it headed west its track crossed the main line on the level at Dundalk Square Crossing. This crossing, which closed in 1954, and the one at Limerick Junction where the Limerick to Waterford line still crosses the Dublin to Cork main line on the level, were the only ones of this type in the whole of Ireland. However, it is doubtful if any passenger trains ever used Barrack Street station as the D&E also opened a station at Dundalk Junction just south of the present station which was also used by D&BJR trains. Barrack Street remained in use for goods traffic until the mid-1990s.

Progress was slow after the line to Castleblayney opened. Ballybay, seven miles on, was not reached until July 1854. Trains began to run as far as Newbliss ten miles beyond Ballybay in August 1855 and through Clones to Lisnaskea by August 1858. Enniskillen was finally reached in February of the following year. There was just one branch off the Dundalk to Enniskillen line. This line opened in 1860 from Shantonagh Junction near Ballybay to Cootehill seven and a half miles away. The D&E's original idea had been to extend this to Cavan to make a junction with the Midland Great Western's line which had reached that town in 1856, branching off the MGWR Dublin to Sligo route at the place which was originally called Cavan Junction but was renamed Inny Junction after 1878. Opposition from the Ulster Railway which had its own plans to reach Cavan put paid to this and the branch was never extended beyond Cootehill.

Mention of the UR here brings us to the other component in this network of lines in the south of the northern province. While strictly speaking the line from Portadown to Clones was not part of the Irish North, both its traffic and its eventual fate were linked to it and it would be pedantic to leave it out of the picture. The original intention of the UR as stated in its prospectus published as early as 1835 was for a line from Belfast to Armagh, but it was clear from the statements of directors and supporters of the company at that time and oft repeated afterwards that their ultimate objective was to take the line further west beyond Armagh. The building of the route to Dublin was to be left to others. The history of Irish railway companies in the nineteenth century is frequently one of disappointing financial performance. Many of the smaller Irish companies were operating close to insolvency and some, such as Bagenalstown & Wexford discussed in Chapter 5, did go bankrupt. Others were bailed out with government loans. The UR was a notable exception to this bleak picture. The consistent performance of UR shares in the four decades of its independent existence when half yearly dividends of up to 7 per cent were not uncommon was testament to the wisdom of its original promoters and their single-minded determination to go west. The difficult economic conditions in the immediate aftermath of the Famine did slow down the UR's progress and it was not until 1858 that the line from Armagh was extended to Monaghan and it was 1863 before it reached Clones and made a junction with the D&E. In 1862 another line reached Clones, making this town on the Monaghan-Fermanagh border an important junction and a major regional railway centre. This was the Clones & Cavan Extension Railway which had been built by the D&E but was largely funded by the UR, the D&BJR and the Dublin & Drogheda. This route, which ensured that a good deal of the traffic to Cavan would pass over UR metals, was the reason the company had objected to the D&E's planned extension of the Cootehill branch.

Meanwhile, over in the north-west, the progress of the Londonderry & Enniskillen had not been rapid. The line to Strabane was scarcely long enough to be viable and even over that short distance of 14 miles the railway had competition for goods traffic. This came in the form of what an old ballad described as 'the mighty fleet that ploughed the deep, from Derry to Strabane'. This was a satirical reference to the Strabane canal which had opened in 1796 and ran for four miles, linking the town to the tidal reaches of the Foyle. The terminus of the railway in Derry was moved about a mile closer to the centre of the city in 1850 when a new station was opened at Foyle Road, close to the Carlisle Bridge over the river, and the other end of the line was extended from Strabane to Newtownstewart and Omagh in the course of 1852.

The following year saw the L&E's tracks struggle forward seven more miles to the small village of Fintona where there was another pause for breath. This allowed one of the most charming of railway oddities in a country which had plenty of contenders in that category to enter the stage. Services began to run as far as the village of Fintona in June 1853 but when construction resumed it was from a spot about three-quarters of a mile short of that original temporary terminus. The company obtained permission from the Board of Trade to work the branch to Fintona from what now became Fintona Junction by horse traction—a state of affairs that continued for the next 104 years during which time the Fintona horse tram, with accommodation for all three classes of passengers, was hauled by a succession of geldings who sedately plodded up and down the branch providing a connection with trains arriving at the junction.

The country between Omagh and Enniskillen is hilly and the line weaved around these hills as Stephenson struggled to find a reasonably level route for the track. It opened to the next station, Dromore, in January 1854 and finally reached Enniskillen in August of that year. One consequence of the topography and the course of the line that this dictated was that the station serving Dromore was about a mile and a half from the village and Trillick station was over two miles distant from its village. In the 1870s Dromore was renamed more accurately Dromore Road to avoid confusion with another GNR station of the same name on the line to Banbridge which had opened in 1863, but there was no clue in the name of Trillick station hinting at its distance from the place it purported to serve.

The L&E had finally reached its objective but it was an isolated and far from prosperous railway. In 1855 the contractor for the whole line, William McCormick, was still owed money by the company and other creditors were also pressing for payment. The L&E flirted with bankruptcy but an Act of 1856 allowed it to raise additional capital through the issue of preference stock which eased its pressing financial problems. Its situation was not helped by some of the locomotives it acquired which included a number of small, four-wheeled well-tank engines which even by the standards of the time must have been totally inadequate for a line over 60 miles long. These machines were described by E.L. Ahrons, a leading authority on steam locomotives writing in *Railway Magazine* in October 1926, as being little better than 'steam perambulators'. Salvation for the L&E came with the belated arrival of the D&E at Enniskillen in 1859. Firstly a new station was built serving both lines and then an Act was passed authorising the D&E to lease the L&E for a term of 99 years. The rather generous terms of the lease produced enough revenue to enable the L&E to pay dividends to its stock holders and it remained in existence as a separate company until 1883 when the GNR finally bought out the lease.

It made good sense to operate the whole Dundalk to Derry line as one unit though it meant that the original name of the D&E was now inappropriate, so in 1862 an Act was passed which changed its name to that of the Irish North Western Railway. The name stuck even after the advent of the GNR in 1876. The first flourish of the new company was to back the Enniskillen & Bundoran Railway which was incorporated in 1861 with the intent of building a 35 mile long line to the town of Bundoran on the Atlantic coast at the southernmost tip of County Donegal. In 1862 the company was granted powers to continue the line to Sligo and changed its name to the Enniskillen, Bundoran & Sligo to mark this. The new line diverged from the Enniskillen to Omagh line at what became known as Bundoran Junction in the district of Kilskerry. A station had existed here called Lowtherstown Road, and later Irvinestown Road, from 1854, but it took on its final name when the branch opened in March 1866. Irvinestown now got its own station on the Bundoran line, three and a half miles from the Junction.

A financial crisis on the London markets in 1866 badly affected railway stocks and may have been the reason why the Sligo extension was never built. As will be noted from other parts of this book, given the amount of money poured into highly speculative railway projects towards the end of the nineteenth century, it is one of the tragedies of Irish railway history that the short 20 mile long line from Bundoran to Sligo along a benign stretch of low-lying land was never built. Bundoran was and is a town of one long main street which runs parallel to the coast. Bundoran station, located off the main street at the end of Railway Road, was ideally placed to allow the line to be extended towards Sligo. Had this occurred, it would ultimately have been part of a railway linking Derry to Limerick and Rosslare which might even have bestowed on it some chance of salvation when it came to the disastrous events of 1957. If such a line were around today, the EU would love it and would probably be pouring money into it as part of a major strategic transport link between the north and south of the island. As it was, Bundoran remained the terminus at the end of the long branch from Bundoran Junction. Although the railway brought at least a measure of prosperity during the summer season, making it an easily accessible destination for both holiday makers and day trippers, it had no strategic significance beyond this.

The final part of this network of lines again owes much to the influence of the Ulster Railway. In 1847 a scheme called the Portadown & Dungannon Railway was promoted to build a line from a junction at Portadown with the UR's route to Armagh, which was close to completion at that time, to the County Tyrone town of Dungannon 15 miles to the west. Nothing happened for several years and the company's parliamentary powers lapsed and had to be renewed in 1853. In 1855 construction began, with the contract being given to the English firm of Fox, Henderson & Co whose explosive activities in County Cork are noted elsewhere (see page 125). The contractors went bankrupt in 1856 and William Dargan had to be invited in to pick up the pieces. Trains began running to a temporary station outside Dungannon while the tunnel which the local landowner insisted on having built (see page 7) was completed. With the encouragement of the UR, the P&D obtained an Act in 1858 to extend the line to a junction with the L&E at Omagh. The Portadown, Dungannon & Omagh company was authorised to raise £100,000 in shares and another £33,000 in loans to drive the 27 mile long line through the foothills of the Sperrin Mountains via Donaghmore, Pomeroy and Carrickmore. Between Dungannon and Sixmilecross the line was heavily graded in both directions. The steepest section of Carrickmore bank, which had to be faced by trains heading east, was as stiff as 1 in 72. The line which the UR operated opened in September 1861, and in 1875 the UR took a 999-year lease on it. The people of Derry now had a second route to Belfast, in competition with the existing line along the north-west coast. The latter had only just been completed as far as through traffic was concerned the previous year when the opening of the bridge over the River Bann at Coleraine connected the separate lines from Belfast and Londonderry which had previously terminated there on either side of the river.

With the exception of a couple of relatively insignificant branches this network of lines in mid and south Ulster was now complete. The lines linking Portadown to Clones and Derry and from there to Dundalk had taken just under 20 years to build. For the record the branch lines were those from Dungannon to Cookstown which served the Tyrone coalfield and opened in 1879, that from Ballyhaise on the Cavan to Clones line to Belturbet dating from 1885 and the line from Inniskeen Junction to Carrickmacross which followed the next year. The UR operated the routes from Portadown to Omagh and Clones; the rest of the lines were in the hands of the INWR. The distance of the INWR main line from Dundalk to Derry was 121 miles. In addition the company worked the Bundoran branch and the independent Finn Valley Railway from Strabane to Stranorlar which opened in 1863 and much later was converted to the 3 ft gauge to become an important part of County Donegal's once extensive system of narrow gauge lines. The INWR was also closely involved in the promotion of the railways to the port of Greenore which are dealt with in Chapter 4, though its impoverished financial condition led to those lines being taken over by the English London & North Western Railway.

Despite the size of the undertaking, the INWR was never a profitable concern. It was forced to go to parliament in 1864 to seek permission to restructure its capital and extinguish substantial arrears of unpaid dividends in the face of what the Act described as the company's 'condition of pecuniary embarrassment'. The cost of building and working a lengthy line through primarily agricultural and not very populous districts with little prospect of traffic increasing substantially debilitated the INWR. The terms of its lease of the L&E did not help matters either.

For years there had been discussions about amalgamating some of the railways in this part of Ireland. It seemed absurd to many that three independent companies were still responsible for working the Dublin to Belfast line—this was surely not the best way to run that railway. While the D&D, D&BJR and the INWR were amenable to a coming together, the problem was the UR which was much more profitable than its neighbours. There was no incentive, indeed there were many disincentives discouraging UR shareholders from having anything to do with their less fortunate counterparts who held stock in the other companies. No general agreement could be reached so in the end the D&D and the D&BJ acted independently and in March 1875 they came together to form the Northern Railway Company (Ireland), with the INWR joining the new concern in January 1876. In April 1876, the UR finally relented and a new company with a new name, one which would be synonymous with progress, enterprise and innovation for the next eight decades, entered the lexicon of Irish railways, the Great Northern Railway (Ireland), the last word being added to distinguish it from its eponymous and equally distinguished English counterpart.

The UR directors drove a hard bargain. Each £100 of UR stock was converted to GNR shares to the value of £124 10 shillings. D&D shareholders got par and those in the D&BJ got £77 10 shillings for their £100. Pity the poor unfortunates who had invested in the INWR. Preference stock holders at least got half the value of their shares but ordinary shareholders only received £5 in GNR shares for every £100 of INWR stock they held, though by this stage you would fancy that many of them would be glad of it and the prospect of at last getting a dividend, even if the capital value of their investment had to be greatly diminished to achieve this. While GNR shareholders did not do as well as those who had held stock in the UR, the company was consistently profitable and paid dividends on ordinary shares of at least 5 per cent until the start of the 1920s. Thereafter a dividend of 3 per cent was maintained throughout the rest of that difficult decade, though even this modest return fell away as economic conditions worsened in the bleak 1930s.

It took a while for the newly formed GNR to get into its stride. A total of 41 directors had sat on the respective boards of the companies that had amalgamated. The first GNR board had 29 directors. As an instrument to manage the company's diverse activities it was as unwieldy and probably as argumentative as a contemporary European Union summit. Added to the top-heavy board was a plethora of locomotive superintendents, civil engineers and traffic managers, all defending their fiefs. The UR seems to have carried on much as before in the guise of the Northern Division of the new company. It was not until 1885 when the UR's long-serving locomotive superintendent John Eaton finally retired that all the GNR locomotives came under the control of one engineer and the UR's red livery began to be phased out. This new man was James C. Park who came from the English GNR. He built the new central workshop complex at Dundalk and from his first locomotive designs a distinctive GNR house style was developed. GNR locomotives built from the 1880s through to the company's last steam engines delivered in 1948 all bore a striking and attractive family resemblance.

The GNR prospered. The larger scale of its operations made for greater economy. The company had a policy of standardisation in relation to its locomotives. Goods and passenger types often had the same type of boiler and many other parts in common. Different wheel sizes and wheel arrangements delivered speed for the passenger engines or power for the goods locomotives. The company's carriages were among the most comfortable in Ireland, and from the 1890s onwards the GNR became one of the first companies in these islands to use electricity to light its carriages. This was at a time when the other companies were using gas. The presence of pressurised gas containers under railway carriages led to some horrific fires in the wake of accidents in England at the turn of the century when the gas escaping from containers fractured in the smash was ignited by coals from the locomotive.

The GNR's policy of standardisation extended beyond its trains to the design of many of its stations and even to the appearance of the houses it built for its station masters. The long-serving GNR civil engineer W.H. Mills who held that post from 1877 to 1909 was responsible for rebuilding many stations in a lovely glazed yellow brick of which those at Lisburn, Dundalk and Malahide are still fine examples. An interesting variation on these survives at Belturbet where cut stone was used to build the station rather than the usual glazed brick. Wooden waiting shelters of standard design began to crop up at stations all over the system. Survivors of these are on the up (Dublin bound) platform at Gormanstown and the down platform at Malahide and one has been preserved at the site of Trew & Moy station in County Tyrone on the erstwhile Derry Road.

With its core of profitable lines, those linking Belfast to Dublin and Derry, the less remunerative parts of the GNR, its inheritance from the INWR in the main, were worked more economically and had value in the traffic they fed on to the rest of the network. As was the case with most lines in Ireland, with the exception of those few which provided commuter services into Dublin and Belfast, the number of passenger trains that operated daily on these GNR lines was never great. The distance from Dundalk to Omagh was just under 88 miles and that from Belfast to Derry about 100. The two routes had a different character in that while one was a secondary main line linking two substantial urban centres the other was a meandering cross-country route serving a large number of small towns and villages along the way.

There was a certain stability to the timetable over the years, with patterns of service which were established early in the history of the two lines more or less maintained throughout their existence. On the Derry Road in 1900, each day there were five trains down from Belfast and four up in the other direction, along with a late-running mail train in the evening in each direction which did not arrive at its destination until early the following morning. Most trains in each direction took about 3 hours. Derry was one of the few places in Ireland which had two railway companies competing for traffic to the same destination, in this case Belfast. Even though the B&NCR route from York Road in Belfast to its Waterside station in Londonderry was a few miles shorter than the GNR line and was less taxing for the locomotives in terms of its gradients, the best trains were not any quicker than those on the GNR as they still took three hours or more for the journey. This was partly due to trains from Belfast having to reverse at Greenisland on the Larne line before heading north. When this impediment was removed in the 1930s with a direct line built over new concrete viaducts at Bleach Green near Whiteabbey, this line produced some of the fastest point-to-point times ever scheduled with steam traction in Ireland, eclipsing times on the GNR line to Derry.

Back in 1900 there were also two daily through trains from Derry to Dundalk, though additional connections at least part of the way were provided from Omagh. There were three through trains in the opposite direction. Speeds were not great on the Irish North and the many station stops slowed matters up even further. For example, the 4.15pm train from Dundalk took 4 hours and 50 minutes to travel the 121 miles to Derry, calling at almost every station on the way.

Moving on 50 years to the GNR timetable which came into operation in September 1950, on the Derry Road there were now five through trains in each direction but it is noticeable that the trains took longer than they had 50 years before. The fastest train from Derry was the 3.50pm restaurant car express which took 3 hours and 10 minutes to complete its journey. One reason for the tardiness of this and other trains was the lengthy station stops at Strabane, Omagh and Portadown which in the case of this service added 24 minutes to the schedule. The services would have been even slower but for the use of railcars to provide most of the stopping services between Omagh and Dungannon. The railcars also called at some of the level crossings along the way where passengers would climb up and down on the railcar's steps. Level crossings proliferated along the railways of Ireland. On the 26 miles between Omagh and Dungannon there were no less than ten. Some were named after the townlands in which they were situated such as Tattykeeran, Edenderry and Garvaghy (there were actually two there: Garvaghy No 1 and No 2 less than a mile apart), while others bore the names of the families who had been their original custodians such as Reynold's and Brimmage's crossings, both between Pomeroy and Donaghmore.

By 1950 the pattern of service on the Irish North had changed somewhat from the beginning of the century in that there were no through trains from Dundalk to Derry, though connections to that city were provided by Belfast to Derry services from Omagh. On the original D&E section, there were only two through trains from Dundalk to Enniskillen, one of which ventured as far as Omagh, though there was a decent service of five or six trains between Omagh and Enniskillen. As this was the winter timetable, Bundoran had only two trains in each direction, though the resort had a better service during the summer months including the fabled *Bundoran Express* of which more anon. As was the case on parts of the Derry Road, the GNR used railcars to provide services from some level crossings of which there were many to choose from on the Irish North, with about 40 alone on the 62-mile stretch from Dundalk Junction to Enniskillen. There is a kind of poetry and a wealth of heritage in their names: Drumgoose, Killygraggy, Sallaghy, Castlebalfour, Lisnagole and many others. Often they carried alternative, semi-official names—those of the families who lived in the little cottages provided by the company beside the level crossings and who looked after them for the house and a trifle of money, opening and closing the gates before and after the passage of the trains, day and night, on every day of the year.

This tracery of level crossings along the railways of Ireland tells its own story about the way many of these lines were built and financed. Building a level crossing and a house for the gate keeper would have used up less of the company's precious capital than erecting a bridge. In truth, apart from local traffic, there were not many vehicles on the roads and the coming of the railways would have reduced this even more. Level crossings only became a nuisance in the later twentieth century, as anyone left drumming on the steering wheel in places such as the Merrion gates in Dublin or in the centre of Lurgan will testify.

The story of the GNR in the first half of the twentieth century is similar to that of the rest of Ireland's railways. The golden age of prosperity faded quickly into the quagmire of civil and political disorder which followed the Great War. With partition, the company found itself in the situation where its tracks now crossed an international frontier in 17 different places. What was probably worse in the long term was the disruption that the border caused to the trade routes which the railways had been built to reflect. Whereas before merchants in towns like Clones and Monaghan would have looked towards Belfast, following the trade route provided by the Ulster Railway in the previous century, with different tariff regimes now in operation and forms to fill in to import and export goods it became simpler for many of them to look south. The trade depression of the 1930s and De Valera's so called economic war with Britain further helped to loosen old ties.

Against this background the threat from the roads also got into gear. In the 1920s unregulated private buses and lorries served virtually every town and village in Ulster. Both governments passed legislation to allow their railway companies to run road services in 1927 and the GNR began to buy up buses and lorries from private operators on either side of the border. The establishment of the Northern Ireland Road Transport Board in 1935 effectively reversed this legislation north of the border and prevented the GNR and the other railway companies from operating road services in the province. However, in the south GNR buses continued to operate, connecting districts not served by the company's railways and feeding traffic on to the railway.

The concept of an integrated public transport network, which is frequently discussed by politicians and environmentalists today, was being operated by the GNR close to 80 years ago. It is all set out in any GNR timetable from the 1950s which lists the close to 100 bus routes operated by the company, not to mention steamer connections across the Irish Sea and, by that stage, even details of Aer Lingus and British European Airways flights from Dublin and Belfast to London, Birmingham, Liverpool, Manchester and the Isle of Man.

Another blow for the company was the bitter three months long railway strike of 1933 which came about when the railway companies imposed wage cuts on their staff. Apart from the loss of income, two malicious derailments occurred during the strike. One of these was on the Derry Road at Omagh Market Branch Junction where the points were tampered with, putting a train from Dungannon to Derry off the rails. Despite all the complications of the border and the difficult economic conditions of the 1930s, the GNR and its routes came through those difficult years intact though with revenue falling all the time. Some sections of double track on the Derry Road and between Armagh and Clones were singled as an economy measure and the company also began to experiment with diesel railcars and railbuses to provide a more economical way of operating some passenger services. However, the coming of the Second World War in 1939 completely changed the landscape in which the company was operating.

Petrol rationing took all but a few essential users' cars off the roads for the duration on both sides of the border. Goods and passenger traffic which had been lost to the roads began to flow back on to the Great Northern and the rest of the Irish railway network. Tonnages of goods carried and the numbers of passengers using the trains both soared. In Northern Ireland the railways briefly came back into favour, seen as strategically important for the war effort. The ports and airfields of Northern Ireland were vital in the Battle of the Atlantic waged against the

German U-boats, and many thousands of American GIs were based there, training for the Allied landings in Europe. On a more practical level this meant the railways had adequate supplies of coal and did not have the crippling coal shortages that the GSR had to endure. Those northern counties of the Free State served by the GNR lines which crossed the border benefited from much better rail services during the Emergency than the rest of the country as a consequence. On the other hand, food and almost everything else was strictly rationed in the north.

Much of what was virtually unobtainable, legally, in Northern Ireland, was freely available south of the border. Smuggling, a new industry which had been created by partition and about the only one that had flourished as a consequence of it, now became more popular than ever. Tales which were handed down in my own family from this period range from the bizarre involving swans 'acquired' around Lough Erne being passed off as turkeys in the run up to Christmas to cheap excursion tickets to Bundoran offered to the citizens of Omagh in the middle of winter. War is a terrible thing: this was the last place anyone from Omagh would normally have wanted to go in December. It was the prospect of being able to buy tea, butter and other contraband rather than winter sunshine and a dip in the Atlantic breakers which brought this extra traffic to the trains of the Irish North.

The apparent antipathy towards the railways in government circles in Northern Ireland which seems to have been in place from before the formation of the NIRTB in 1935 was not extinguished completely by wartime fuel rationing if this story which my father loved to tell is anything to go by. A large quantity of flour was stored in sacks underneath the Town Hall in Omagh where he worked, to ensure food supplies for the local population and any evacuees from other areas in the event of an enemy attack. There was a problem with vermin attacking the supplies and this was duly notified to the relevant department in Stormont. Some time later a gentleman appeared from Belfast, having driven all the way in his car. This was at a time when there was a perfectly adequate train service, and petrol was strictly rationed due to enemy action. His first enquiry related not to the problem with the food supplies, but as to the location of the best hotel in town. After a good lunch he condescended to inspect the sacks and having conducted this important war work he drove off back to Belfast. Officialdom soon swung into action and the fate of the Town Hall mice was sealed: a parcel arrived a week later containing a dozen mousetraps. At a time when sailors were risking their lives every day to bring fuel across the Atlantic in the convoys, such a monstrous waste of a precious resource by some jobsworth was inexcusable.

For good or ill, the railway made Bundoran just as it made Portrush, Newcastle, Tramore, Kilkee and other towns around the coast of Ireland which flourished as a destination for day trippers and holiday makers from the turn of the last century onwards. As discussed elsewhere, all the Irish railways made great efforts to promote tourism and the GNR was no exception. At Bundoran, the Great Northern's hotel surrounded by its golf course high on the cliffs above the seashore was a dominant landmark in the town and special tickets were offered to golfers which included both rail travel and their green fees. In its advertisements at the turn of the nineteenth century the GNR proudly boasted that the hotel was lit by electricity, though by that time the GNR was already using this to illuminate at least some of its carriages. Golf and electric light, as we will observe later in County Mayo, seem to have been major attractions for the well-heeled Edwardian tourist as were hot and cold sea and fresh water baths, another recurring theme, which were also available at the GNR hotel. An advertisement for the Bundoran hotel dating from 1900 assures the public, and I quote: *The sanitary arrangements are perfect.* That's all we need to know then, get the *Bradshaw's Guide* down from the bookshelf, to hell with the Riviera, we're off to Bundoran this summer.

To enable the hoi polloi who could not afford such wonders and almost certainly had to endure less than perfect sanitary arrangements at home to at least gaze in awe at the Great Northern's hotel, perched imperiously high above the beach, there was always the Sunday excursion to Bundoran, timed to leave after the churches had done their business. This was a regular diversion for many in Omagh and other towns and villages on or in reach of the Irish North. For a modest outlay families could have a day on the beach and young ones could indulge in what young ones like to indulge in away from the disapproving gaze of their elders. Another major incentive to head for the station after church was that it provided many citizens, of all denominations it must be said, with a means of escape from the joyless and alcohol-less gulag that was the Ulster Sabbath which was officially, if not always in practice, 'dry'. Even though I was only a toddler when the line closed and I cannot claim to remember travelling on it, I have a vague memory of a drunk man singing on a train, which sort of ties in with the above. There is also a tragic personal memory in my family with which the line will always be associated. My father's brother, the man I was named after, a gifted amateur musician and a printer by trade, took an ordinary Sunday excursion to Bundoran early in the season in 1938, caught a chill there which developed into pneumonia and died soon afterwards at too young an age. On a brighter note, over three decades later, my first girlfriend had a summer job in a café on Railway Road, so there was still a bit of action for at least one railway enthusiast down there long after the line had closed.

Another railway story handed down in the family concerned a different uncle who was friendly with a policeman in the town. One day the policeman insisted he come up to the railway station with him at a specific time. Shortly after they got there, a train from Derry arrived and the policeman led my uncle down the platform before stopping in front of one compartment. He then nudged Uncle Paddy and pointed to the man in the carriage and said, 'That's Pierrepoint the hangman. He executed a man in Derry jail this morning.' I am sure many reading this will have stories such as these in their own family history relating to the railways from the era when they played such a significant part in the daily life of towns and villages all over the country.

Returning to the Irish North, it would be impossible to recount the history of its later years without referring to one of its great claims to fame in that it was traversed by one of the few named trains ever to run in Ireland, the *Bundoran Express*. The name was first used before the war but it came into its own in the years after it. The purpose of the train, which only operated during the summer, was twofold. It was used by holiday makers heading to the seaside but its main function was more spiritual in that it conveyed the faithful to do penance at St Patrick's Purgatory, a holy site on an island in Lough Derg in County Donegal near Pettigo. There they would walk around on their bare feet for three days fasting, living on bread and water and doing a lot of praying. Holiday makers with excited kids and those intent on spiritual fulfilment and eternal salvation made up the strange mix of travellers who filled the compartments of the carriages of the *Bundoran Express*. The train left Dublin usually at 8.45am and stopping only at Drogheda arrived in Dundalk around 10.00am. Engines were changed there and the train headed off again along the Irish North running non-stop to Clones where a through coach from Belfast was added before the *Bundoran Express* set off on another non-stop run, this time from Clones to Pettigo, a distance of 45 miles.

In marked contrast to all the other passenger trains on this route which stopped just about everywhere, the *Bundoran Express* even ground at walking pace round the sharp curve through Enniskillen station and the other one at Bundoran Junction. The purpose of this was to avoid stopping in Northern Ireland and subjecting the would-be penitents to yet more misery at the hands of the Customs men. I have never seen any explanation as to why this unprecedented non-stop run took place. There was no logical operational reason for it and one would have thought that the train would have picked up some passengers at Enniskillen had it stopped there. The only semi-plausible reason I have come across was to do with the customs examinations, not so much because of the delays they entailed—the *Bundoran Express* was hardly a flyer—but rather, because of their cost. Even though these delayed services on all cross-border lines, to add insult to injury, the railway companies had to pay the authorities for the privilege of having customs officials crawl all over their passengers and their luggage. As the *Bundoran Express* ran non stop through Northern Ireland it at least escaped this imposition. The village of Pettigo was one which straddled the border but fortunately its station was situated just inside County Donegal thus enabling the *Bundoran Express* to take on the character of a Cold War express from Berlin for that part of its journey.

The war years had brought the GNR back into prosperity; dividends for ordinary shareholders even returned between 1941 and 1947. The company used this boost to its revenues wisely and invested in new steam locomotives in the years after the war and in 1948 put into service the first mainline diesel trains in these islands. The steam locomotives included five new members of the U class light 4-4-0s, which were put to work on the Irish North where they joined the earlier batch of these engines which dated from 1915. The new machines were distinguished from their older sisters by the provision of a larger and more modern looking cab to give greater protection to their crews. By now many of the locomotives used on passenger trains were being turned out from Dundalk works in the GNR's sublime sky blue livery, lined out in black and white, with their frames and buffer beams picked out in red. This was perhaps not the most practical colour scheme for a machine inevitably associated with dirt and ash and smuts but when it was kept clean—and often it was in the company's declining years—it was such an impressive sight.

The good times were not to last and by the start of the 1950s the GNR was heading for the end of the line in a financial sense. The traffic which wartime fuel restrictions had brought back from the roads began to drift away and costs were rising alarmingly. The company was reaching the end of its resources and in November 1950 its directors announced that they could not maintain their services in the New Year. Faced with a complete shut down of a major transport undertaking, the two governments acted swiftly and in a rare example of cross-border co-operation, they bought the GNR for a sum of £4.5 million, both paying equal shares of the purchase price. In order to run the undertaking, Acts were passed in both the Dublin and Belfast parliaments setting up the Great Northern Railway Board. Each jurisdiction appointed five members to this, the roles of chairman and vice chairman alternating between northern and southern appointees. The Board, like the company before it, had a clear strategic vision of where it wanted to go. In particular, diesel trains were to replace steam traction as soon as possible. However, as always with Ireland's railways, finance was the problem. The Board's political masters never gave it the funds to make the necessary investment in a modernisation programme. Some new diesel railcars were bought but they were not provided in sufficient numbers to make a significant difference to the ever increasing losses that were being sustained.

There were inevitably different opinions expressed on either side of the border concerning the new arrangements. In the negotiations leading up to the purchase one interesting proposal put forward by the Dublin government was for the setting up of a national transport authority for the whole country to operate railways, canals and road transport in all the 32 counties. While this may have seemed like a good idea south of the border it was not likely to find favour among Unionist politicians in Belfast. Speaking about this in the Dáil, the leader of the Irish Labour Party, William Norton, rather let the political cat out of the bag when he insisted that this proposal was made 'because it was sound from an economic point of view and because it was one of those independent steps which, ultimately, we must take if we are ever to secure the union of our country from the standpoint of a reunion of minds and hearts as well.'

These sentiments were echoed by Liam Cosgrave who played a minor role in the negotiations to save the GNR. Speaking in the same debate about these negotiations he said, 'I am very pleased that it has been brought to a successful conclusion, not only for the sake of the Great Northern Railway Company and the employees of the company, but because of the goodwill which agreements of this nature generate between the people of this part of the country and our fellow-countrymen in the Six Counties. The goodwill which has been generated by a number of agreements of this nature—the Erne electricity agreement, the Foyle and Bann fisheries agreement, and the Great Northern Railway agreement—must inevitably have reactions on the ultimate reunification of the country.' Honourable sentiments indeed, but hollow words in the light of subsequent developments.

Though the Stormont government played its part in averting the complete closure of the GNR system in 1951, this did not signal a change in the general antipathy towards the province's railways which had emanated from there since the 1930s and the formation of the NIRTB. There were no sinister political motives associated with their conduct in the next few years. Rather the view from Stormont was as detached as that of an accountant looking at a balance sheet. The Unionist government was doggedly following a policy that public transport had to be made to pay its way, as indeed was its counterpart in the south. The biggest loss makers were the railways. Therefore they had to go. This attitude was brutally asserted by a future Prime Minister of Northern Ireland, Brian Faulkner. Speaking at Stormont in March 1956 he said, 'We must apply to each section of railway line a financial test: is it working at a profit, or is it working at a loss? If it is working at a profit then there may be grounds for keeping that service in existence. If it is working at a loss then it ought to be cut out. This may well mean the total elimination of railway services in Northern Ireland. That is a situation which some people might not envisage with any joy or relish, but one which has got to be faced. As a community we cannot afford to subsidise a passenger service which is obviously not wanted by passengers or by freight consigners because they are leaving it in increasing numbers every year.' This opinion was shared by many in his party, and against such attitudes the railways did not stand a chance. These remarks were made in the context of the proposals to close the Irish North but they also anticipated the closure of the Derry Road and the other lines which were abandoned in 1965. I suppose the only crumb of comfort in all of this is that at least a few lines still survive in Northern Ireland. It could have been a whole lot worse.

The losses continued to mount under the stewardship of the GNRB. The prevarication of the two governments over funds to invest in the new diesel trains which the Board wanted to buy only added to these. Piecemeal closures began in 1955 in County Down with the line from Scarva to Banbridge and from there to Newcastle. The following year the Banbridge to Knockmore Junction (Lisburn) line was cut but these were not enough to satisfy the anti-rail lobby that ruled Northern Ireland. In 1956 the Ministry of Commerce announced plans to close all of the Irish North within their jurisdiction and the Portadown to Tynan section of the line to Clones, 115 miles of railway in all. This of course not only affected those parts of the Irish North in Northern Ireland, it rendered the rest of the system in the Republic virtually useless—the 8-mile stump of the Bundoran branch from Belleek to the terminus and the lines from Clones to Monaghan and Dundalk. It also spelled doom for the Sligo, Leitrim & Northern Counties line (see Chapter 3). This was a unilateral decision which ignored the advice of the GNRB, county councils and business and farming organisations across the areas affected by the closures. Under the legislation which set up the Board, these proposals were referred to tribunals north and south of the border. The northern tribunal rubber-stamped the decision, the southern one took the opposite view, but the Stormont government had made its mind up already. Why invest money in what was seen as an outdated and loss-making form of public transport and in the case of the GNR lines, in a network that was viewed as being of most benefit to what Unionist politicians viewed as a foreign country? Sporadic republican violence which was renewed in the mid-1950s can only have added to this mentality. They had a long history of wreaking havoc on the soft targets which the railways were, dating back to the 1916–1923 period. In March 1957 some of these heroes highjacked the night goods from Enniskillen to Derry at Porthall in County Donegal. The unmanned train was sent off to crash into the station at Foyle Road in Derry where fortunately little damage was done.

The debates on the closures at Stormont followed predictable lines. Lord Glentoran the Minister of Commerce, chief villain of the piece, who did not even send a representative to the northern tribunal, claimed the UTA would only need 15 extra lorries and 17 more buses to cope with the additional traffic from the lines to be closed in the counties of Tyrone and Fermanagh. The Nationalist MP for South Fermanagh, Cahir Healey, took a rather different point of view. Speaking at Stormont in June 1957 he said, 'When the Government took over the railways from private control they promised that road and rail transport would be made complementary to one another. If the buses had fed the railways, as was originally intended, and not have started in as competitors of the railways, the lines today would, if dieselised, be paying their way, or very nearly so. Instead, the Ulster Transport Authority officials who were put on the Great Northern Railway Board deliberately ran buses on roads alongside the railway wherever people could be found to travel. New buses in plenty were ordered but no new carriages.' He had a point. This pro-road transport policy had been in place since the NIRTB was set up in the 1930s when the railway companies were prevented from operating their own road vehicles in co-ordination with the trains, allowing those of the NIRTB to run in competition with them.

However, it could and should have turned out very differently. As Lord Glentoran himself pointed out in June 1957, 'When I discussed the matter with Mr Lemass on 25th May his Government had not then come to a decision as to their attitude. I understand now, however, that they, too, have felt unable to support the burden of the losses on these lines which under the terms of the Great Northern Railway Agreement they would have had to do if they had wished them to remain open after 30th September next, and have agreed that the common services should be withdrawn from 1st October.' Even though it pains me to admit it, he was right. Under the terms of the legislation which established the GNRB, the government of the Republic could have kept these lines open by agreeing to cover the losses they were making. Their decision not to do this makes them as complicit in this disaster as Glentoran and his cronies who started the process, but this fact is often forgotten.

CIÉ trains should have been running from Dundalk to Derry after the Board was dissolved in 1958 and its remaining assets were divided between CIÉ and the UTA. One might have thought this would have been attractive to those in Dáil Éireann for political if not necessarily economic reasons, but there was a big gap between the official rhetoric and the reality of spending money to back it up in the form of subsidies for these loss-making cross-border lines much in need of investment in modern rolling stock. By this time the Republic was getting comfortable with partition, and it was probably only those who believed that Irish unity could be achieved by hijacking goods trains and blowing up railway bridges who would have wanted to sign that cheque, or paid in cash as was more likely in their case.

Lord Glentoran made it quite clear in 1957 that he expected the Derry Road would soon go the way of the Irish North. Two years was his preferred interval between the closures. In fact it lingered on for another eight years, some of which I still recall with the greatest of pleasure. Because there were never enough diesel trains to operate all the services, steam engines worked on the line right up to the end. In 1963 the UTA even bought a few ex-GNR steam locomotives from the now fully dieselised CIÉ to keep services running up to closure. The savages of the UTA had already obliterated the beautiful GNR sky blue livery on their own engines with their black paint, but these refugees from the south were still a rhapsody in blue and for one of them, the sublimely beautiful S class 4-4-0 No 171 *Slieve Gullion*, now in the safe hands of the Railway Preservation Society of Ireland, this stay of execution led to her preservation. Every night the goods could be heard struggling up the bank out of Omagh station and there was usually an engine to be found shunting at the station or in the Market Yard goods depot.

A throwback to the *Bundoran Express* also appeared during the summer months when there was a through CIÉ service from Dublin to Omagh via Portadown which brought pilgrims for Lough Derg who were taken by bus the rest of the way from Omagh. The roads, which were supposed to have been improved following the closures of 1957, but never were, provided an additional bit of penance for them on the UTA buses which took them on the final leg of their journey to Lough Derg. This train brought strange looking and sounding CIÉ General Motors built 141 class diesels to Omagh. Later these would be revered as they remained in service well into the new millennium but I still remember with delight that damp day when the rails were greasy and the diesel locomotive on the return working had to get a shove up the bank out of Omagh station by the ex-GNR 0-6-0 based there. It was too good to last and the final rites took place in February 1965 to the sound of detonators exploding under the wheels of the last trains. Tyrone County Council tried to challenge the closure in the courts but it was a futile exercise; the busmen and their political allies had won.

The effect of the closures of the Irish North and the Derry Road was to remove all broad gauge railway passenger services from five counties—Donegal, Tyrone, Fermanagh, Cavan and Monaghan. With the current and seemingly permanently fragile nature of the ecology of the planet, that gap in the railway map of Ireland which the closures of 1957 and 1965 created has condemned perhaps a quarter of the population of the entire island to a complete dependence on road transport, with no realistic alternative to it. At the time they closed, the loss of these lines was frustrating and damaging, but with the passage of time the consequences may take on an even greater significance. As the oil begins to run out or its price escalates to a level that makes our enforced dependence on it economically debilitating, this may cause many who are not railway romantics to join those of us who are mourning the demise of most of the Great Northern Railway in that act of railway vandalism which is almost without parallel in these islands.

Retracing in recent years the former routes of the Irish North and the Derry Road left me feeling terribly depressed, more so than with any of the other lines covered in this book. They were my lines, the ones which my family used and in the case of the Derry Road a line on which I travelled many times as a boy and which formed my life-long passion for all things that run on rails. Over half a century has passed since the crimes of 1957 and it will not be long before the closure of the Derry Road has reached the same melancholy landmark, and yet I was somehow appalled and almost personally offended that so much of these great iron arteries have slipped from view with the passage of time. Omagh and Strabane were once important railway junctions, bustling with passengers and engines shunting, but you would be hard pushed to know it today. New roads follow precisely the course of the old railway through these towns. At least the one in Omagh acknowledges the memory of what it replaced and is called Great Northern Road. Some of the bridges which carried the line across the Rivers Strule and Mourne between Omagh and Sion Mills are still in place but so compromised with over 40 years of growth no longer kept in check by the scythes of the permanent way men and coals from the engines that they are quite hard to view let alone photograph.

There is the odd relic which is more accessible such as the GNR station master's house at Victoria Bridge, the signal in the garden a reminder for the uninitiated of its former glory when the station master was an important figure in the local community. The single-storey station at St Johnston is also in good order and in use as a private residence. Though the GNR station in Derry at Foyle Road, a remarkable Italianate pastiche, like a scaled-down version of the frontage on to Amiens Street of the company's Dublin terminus, has long been demolished, there is a railway museum on the site of the former goods yards beyond Craigavon Bridge. The Foyle Valley Railway Museum has had a chequered history in recent years and the artifacts it contains relate to the narrow gauge railways of neighbouring County Donegal rather than the GNR. Tracks of 3 ft gauge have been laid on part of the formation of the Derry Road south from the city towards the border with County Donegal and see the occasional outing of a preserved County Donegal Railways railcar. It is ironic that the only part of the Derry Road which it is still possible to traverse by rail has been converted to the narrow gauge. Still, any port in a storm.

South of Omagh, the stone arches of the Leap Bridge carry the trackbed over the River Camowen and incredibly, just north of Beragh station, a distant signal still stands sentinel, its yellow arm in the correct position to warn spectral goods trains to slow down for the station up ahead. From the overbridge at Beragh station, a good view of the well maintained station complete with signal box can be obtained without trespassing. Moving on from Beragh, the formation can still be seen in many locations. I was struck how benign-looking today is the green lane which was once Carrickmore bank with its gradients of 1 in 70 and 1 in 80, which must have put the fear of God into many a young fireman as his steam pressure gauge fell on the climb to the second highest point on the whole of the GNR, 561 ft above sea level, between Carrickmore and Pomeroy. Dungannon was, like Omagh and Strabane, once a junction where the branch to Cookstown left the main line, though again you would never know it today and Lord Northland's tunnel is still there, though I did not venture off in search of it. The site of the next station east of Dungannon, Trew & Moy, is an absolute gem. The main station building is in fine condition and nearby there is a GNR wooden waiting shelter flanked by a couple of signals.

The straggling tracks of the Irish North have become even more buried in their landscape—the odd bridge here and there, a line of trees between the drumlins just about marking the course once followed by the *Bundoran Express* and countless other less distinguished workings. It is still clear that Ballybay was once a railway town, its station for once conveniently situated for its citizens in the centre of the town. The main station building and signal cabin are still in existence and a short distance away the GNR station master's house is in beautiful condition. After the Great War the GNR built two large concrete semi-circular engine sheds, called roundhouses, at Portadown Junction and Clones. The latter is still in existence, its original purpose recognisable to the initiated, now converted for industrial use. This and a few other buildings hint at the importance this County Monaghan junction once had.

Perhaps the most melancholy of all the locations I visited is Bundoran Junction, its site marked by the bridge over a minor road from where many a photograph of trains from Bundoran and Omagh heading towards Enniskillen was taken. The main station building is in private hands and in good condition and a GNR waiting shelter can be seen from the bridge as is a name board. The trackbed has been filled in to make it level with the platforms but the place is still clearly Bundoran Junction as recalled from those photos. However, it was the trees which got to me for some reason. Why should I be surprised that there should be mature trees growing on a railwaytrack bed abandoned for over 50 years? *Sic transit gloria mundi,* as I vaguely recall from my Latin classes, almost as distant as the memory of the GNR. The Irish North has almost become archaeology. As it sinks back into the landscape from which it was once hacked out by navvies with their shovels and picks, it is becoming harder and harder to believe it ever existed, but it did and I wish we had it back, and if we could somehow undo that great gap in the railway map of Ireland we would all be the better for it.

Chapter 3

COLLATERAL DAMAGE:
THE FATE OF THE SL&NCR

In 2001 I was involved in the publication of a pictorial book on the Sligo, Leitrim & Northern Counties Railway, that charming and somewhat eccentric line which ran from Enniskillen to Sligo. The book was duly released and was selling well when, about six months after it appeared, one Saturday morning, as I driving up to the local supermarket to get a few bits and pieces I had a phone call. We always kept a skeleton staff in the office on Saturday mornings as many customers found it convenient to order books at that time and my caller had been given my mobile number by one of my colleagues who was manning the phones that morning and knew I was the one best placed to answer this potential customer's enquiry. The gentleman now on the phone to me had only just heard about our SL&NCR book and wanted a bit more information on it. As we began to talk, it turned out that as a young man in the 1950s he had been a guard on the railway for a few short years up to its closure. It is to my eternal shame that I did not keep the man's number and I cannot recall his name, but when the line closed in 1957 he could find no alternative employment in the area and had taken the well-trodden path to England where he had made a good life for himself, though not as I recall on the railways, and had raised a family there.

However, sitting in my car that morning in a supermarket car park in the second year of the new millennium, I was suddenly transported back to the 1950s and to a different world when the SL&NCR was still active and providing a vital transport link for the people in those border counties which it served. Memories, as vivid as if they had happened yesterday, poured through the ether, bringing that long-closed railway line back to life in a way which no picture, no matter how well composed, and no passage of prose, no matter how carefully crafted, could ever do. And even though my friend had probably not been in a brake van for close to fifty years, his recollections of the work and his obvious affection for both the job and the railway he had served were as fresh as if he had just finished a shift on the line that morning.

The railway that had provoked such happy and long-lasting memories was genuinely unique in many different ways. Its history was largely one of a struggle to survive and to retain its independence and yet, not only against all the odds did it manage to do this, its nemesis in 1957 was caused by factors completely beyond its control. The enforced closure of the GNR lines through Enniskillen simply denied the SL&NCR an outlet for its traffic. In thinking about the fate of this railway, I was reminded of that ghastly euphemism favoured by military men in recent times who like to disguise the death and destruction which they wreak on those not directly in their firing line, with the use of that bland yet sinister phrase, collateral damage. The SL&NCR was indeed a victim of collateral damage inflicted at the hands of those who conspired to obliterate all traces of the railway from a large part of the north of Ireland in 1957.

The Sligo, Leitrim & Northern Counties Railway was one of the last in Ireland to be promoted in what might be described in the classic early and mid Victorian mode. There were no government grants or baronial guarantees to assist its construction. Indeed if it had been promoted a few years later the company might well have benefited from such help. The railway was authorised by parliament in 1875, with a share capital of £200,000 and borrowing powers of up to another £100,000. The land-owning class in nineteenth-century Ireland has been rightly vilified for its profligacy and its conduct in the years after the Famine when many thousands of tenants were evicted for the non-payment of rents. However, there are many examples of landowners who did not fit that stereotype, and the men who built the SL&NCR would be in that category. It was a local line borne of local necessity. Those involved in financing it were among the great and good of the area it served, men like two of the Gore-Booths of Lissadell in County Sligo whose family later befriended the young William Butler Yeats. The name of the Gore-Booth's estate, and those of other directors such as Hazelwood and Lurganboy, were perpetuated for many years on some of the line's locomotives.

To help raise the money the Act allowed interest on some of the capital required to be guaranteed by directors and supporters of the line, almost a private version of the baronial guarantee, and the SL&NCR was given permission to pay for some of the land needed to build the line in shares in the company rather than in cash. These were not the actions of grasping capitalists, rather those of men who were anxious to see the line built. Faced with the difficulty of finding a contractor to commence the work, Arthur Tottenham the SL&NCR chairman resigned his post in 1877 to enable him to become a contractor to construct the line.

The first section, the 12 miles from Enniskillen to Belcoo, opened in 1879, leaving over 30 miles to be constructed. To raise more money, a loan of up to £100,000 was sought from the Board of Works but this was only agreed when the directors and some shareholders undertook to guarantee the interest on this. By now the time allowed in the original Act for completion of the line was running out so another Act of Parliament had to be obtained in 1880 to extend the time and allow another £60,000 to be raised in shares or loans. It was not until November 1882 that the line was finally opened throughout and trains could run from Enniskillen to Sligo. The total cost of construction had come to over £340,000 and the impecunious company was also deeply indebted to the Bristol Wagon Company for its rolling stock. Once again the SL&NCR had to turn to its own people to stave off disaster.

Charles Morrison, a major shareholder, settled the debts owed for the company's locomotives, carriages and wagons and hired the stock back to the SL&NCR to enable it to run its services.

For most of the first twenty years of its existence, the company teetered on the brink of insolvency. While receipts exceeded the cost of running the railway the debt owed to the Board of Works was a particular problem and this forced the company into receivership from 1890 to 1897. The attitude of the Treasury towards the SL&NCR was quite harsh. It seemed overly keen to rid itself of the company in order to get its money back, and in 1894 officials engaged in negotiations to sell the line to the MGWR and the GNR for as little as £120,000. The directors of the SL&NCR were rightly outraged at this as were local people who saw the line as competition to the bigger companies, with the positive effect on rates and charges which that was likely to produce. It must have galled the SL&NCR directors that at a time when the Treasury was pursuing them vigorously for repayment of its debts, it was dishing out generous grants to other railways, notably the nearby line from Claremorris to Collooney which was the beneficiary of both guarantees and grants. In their negotiations with the Treasury and the Board of Works the SL&NCR directors argued that had they any inkling at the time they were struggling to raise the money to build their line of the government largess which followed on from the passing of the Tramways Act of 1883, at first in the form of baronial guarantees and latterly in outright grants for railway construction, they would have postponed the promotion of their line for a few years to reap this harvest.

This dispute occurred against a background of widespread dissatisfaction directed towards the Irish railway companies at the turn of the nineteenth century. There were frequent demands that they should be nationalised because of the excessive rates which they appeared to be levying on the carriage of goods. Some went so far as to see this as an impediment to the development of the whole Irish economy. Speaking in the House of Commons in

February 1893, William Field who represented the St Patrick constituency in Dublin claimed that the Irish companies charged rates which were between 10 and 20 per cent higher than their counterparts in England. Indeed the majority report of the government's own Vice-Regal Commission into Ireland's railways, published in 1910, advocated that the whole network should be taken into public ownership.

In the end a settlement was reached in 1897 with the Board of Works which saw interest payments reduced and rescheduled. The SL&NCR also at last regained ownership of its rolling stock. Despite the complaints about the way it had been financed, the opening of the Claremorris to Collooney line in 1895 was likely to provide a boost to the SL&NCR's traffic. Back in 1884, when that line was first mooted, the promoters had approached SL&NCR to work it. That scheme was abandoned, but when it was revived in the early 1890s the working of the new line was entrusted to the Waterford & Limerick Railway. In 1896, to reflect more accurately the huge area served by lines it either owned or worked, which now stretched from Waterford to Sligo, that company changed its title to the Waterford, Limerick & Western. The arrival of the line from the south also endowed the village of Collooney with its third separate station, dictated by geography as much as anything else, because the original MGWR Dublin to Sligo line approached Collooney at a higher level than the other two. It also led to the building of a connection from the Claremorris line to the SL&NCR. This passed under the MGWR line and made an east-facing junction with the SL&NCR, the direction the anticipated livestock trains to and from the great western fairs were expected to roll.

By the start of the new century, the financial condition of the SL&NCR had stabilised, and with the opening of the connection to the Claremorris line it had reached its final route mileage. Several schemes were promoted in the years before 1914 which might have affected the line but none of these were built. The first was the great mad folly of a scheme which had the title of the

Ulster & Connaught Light Railway, first promoted in 1903. If its megalomaniac plans had been realised it would have resulted in a narrow gauge railway stretching across the middle of Ireland, running virtually coast to coast from Newry or Greenore in the east to a western terminus in County Galway. There was also to be a branch to the River Shannon at Rooskey in County Leitrim. It would have absorbed all or part of the existing Newry & Bessbrook Tramway and the Clogher Valley and Cavan & Leitrim railways, in addition to building many more miles of new 3 ft gauge track. It is a reflection on the lack of any alternative to the railway as an effective means of inland transport before the Great War that such a scheme was taken seriously at the time. The landscape changed so quickly after the war that less than 20 years after the U&C was first mooted it would have appeared to any realistic observer as a hopelessly impractical scheme. Even the most fanatical of railway enthusiasts might have shuddered at the prospect of having to spend maybe eight hours in a rattling narrow gauge carriage to make an unlikely odyssey from Newry to Rooskey. A more realistic option for the SL&NCR was the proposal drawn up by independent promoters for a broad gauge branch from Dromahair to Arigna to tap the traffic emanating from the coal mines in the Arigna valley. The SL&NCR offered to work such a line but no government money was forthcoming and it was never built. The mines at Arigna continued to be served by a branch of the Cavan & Leitrim Railway and this traffic helped to keep that line in business until the late 1950s.

When the first part of the SL&NCR opened for passenger traffic in March 1879, three trains were offered each way between Enniskillen and Belcoo. This pattern was extended to Sligo when the whole line opened in 1882, with trains leaving Enniskillen at 9.15am, 1.20 and 7.15pm. In the other direction departures from Sligo were at 5.30 and 10.30am and 3.50pm. Soon after opening a timetable evolved which offered four services in each direction along the whole length of the lines. *Baird's Irish Railway and Steamship Guide*, published in August 1900, shows trains leaving

Sligo at 6.00 and 10.15am, 3.30 and 4.20pm. From Enniskillen departures for Sligo were at 6.00 and 10.10am, 1.35 and 6.40pm. What the published timetable does not show is that some of the trains were mixed, that is, they conveyed both passenger carriages and goods wagons. Journey times for the 48 miles varied from 2 hours 15 minutes to some 3 hours 35 minutes for the 4.20pm departure from Sligo which needed the extra time to shunt wagons on and off the train at stations along the way. The two quickest services were the Mail trains, the mid-morning passenger train from Sligo and the early afternoon departure from Enniskillen which provided connections to and from steamers crossing the Irish Sea from the ports of Dublin and Belfast and for a time, Greenore. Such was the stability of the timetable, when the railway was paid compensation by the Free State government for carriages destroyed in attacks during the Civil War, one of three fine bogie coaches bought with the money was not fitted with electric lighting as it was meant to be used only on these trains and therefore would not need to run in the dark.

The SL&NCR's most important traffic was livestock and it could be said that it was the Englishman's love of his roast beef which kept the railway in business throughout the eight decades of its existence. In our own times when so much of the meat produced in Ireland is slaughtered and processed here, it is perhaps hard to appreciate just how important was the export of live cattle well within living memory. Most Irish railways had a share of this trade and made great efforts to work it expeditiously to ensure the welfare of the beasts in transit. Cattle specials from all over the extensive GS&WR network converged on the sidings at Cabra close to Smithfield in Dublin for the Thursday market, and the MGWR lines from the west were also busy for decades with trains of livestock for the export market. On the SL&NCR, while cattle wagons were conveyed on ordinary goods and mixed trains, there was provision in the timetable for special trains to be run as required. The flow was almost always loaded wagons heading east, with the empty stock going in the other direction. At the time the line closed even though the wagon stock had been depleted, cattle wagons accounted for nearly half the total number of goods vehicles on the company's books. Many of the cattle came from fairs in Mayo and Galway served by the line south from Collooney to Claremorris and Athenry. Livestock was loaded as the fairs wound down in the afternoon and taken north to Collooney where the beasts would be detrained, fed, watered and held overnight before transfer into SL&NCR wagons for the journey east. Loaded trains could be destined for Belfast, Derry or Greenore and were handed over to the GNR at Enniskillen where they would arrive in the late afternoon. This allowed sufficient time for the wagons to be remarshalled as required, to be taken forward to the ports in time for the overnight sailings to England or Scotland.

As mentioned above, the SL&NCR suffered some disruption during the Civil War. In March 1923 Carrignagat signal box, which controlled the junction with the Sligo line, was destroyed in an arson attack, but the most alarming incident took place on 3 April of that year when a passenger train was derailed between Manorhamilton and Glenfarne, with the locomotive rolling down an embankment in the process. Because the line crossed into Northern Ireland, the SL&NCR did not become part of the GSR in 1925 and remained independent, though with partition Customs Posts were soon established at Belcoo and Glenfarne stations on either side of the border. The 1930s was a difficult decade for the company. Services were disrupted during a bitter 12-week long strike in Northern Ireland in 1933, and later the same year a bus service began to operate between Enniskillen and Sligo for the first time.

Worse was to follow. The so-called economic war between the Free State and Britain resulted in punitive tariffs being levied by the British government on cattle imported from the Free State, potentially disastrous for a line so dependent on this traffic. Also in 1933, expenditure began to creep ahead of receipts for the first time. This in turn led to the first subsidy from the government of Northern Ireland to offset the effects on the company of the tariff war. Coming from a regime that was so blatantly anti-railway for so long, this subsidy, which was called Grant-In-Aid, to a company which operated predominantly in what those in Stormont would have viewed as a foreign country, continued to be paid into the 1950s. It was recognition of the importance of the cattle trade in those border counties. Indeed it was even paid during the years of the Second World War when the finances of the SL&NCR improved and its revenue was greater than expenditure. In this brief window of prosperity which benefited railway operators on both sides of the border and allowed them to return to profit as a consequence of the virtual elimination of private cars and lorries from the roads of the country due to wartime fuel shortages, the annual Grant-In-Aid from Stormont was equal to the company's operating profit.

When services resumed after the 1933 strike, only two passenger trains now ran daily each way instead of the previous three. In an effort to return the passenger service to what it had been, while at the same time reducing operating costs, in June 1934 the SL&NCR used a railbus for the first time. This was literally a road bus converted to run on rails. The railbus was developed by the GNR as a means of providing a passenger service on lightly used lines where the costs associated with using steam locomotives to provide such a service could not be justified. The key to the success of the railbus was the ingenious invention of two engineers based at Dundalk works, Howden and Meredith, who designed a new type of wheel which combined the steel flange of a conventional rail vehicle with a pneumatic tyre which made the ride much smoother. Without the rubber component of the wheel cushioning the impact of the track on this very light vehicle the railbus would have been shaken to bits in a short space of time. The first railbus was introduced by the GNR in 1934 and it proved so economical that the SL&NCR arranged to have one of its own built at Dundalk works. A GNR petrol-engined AEC road bus was converted and, as Railbus A, it began to operate on the line in June 1935. It could seat 32 passengers and hauled a lightweight trailer which was used for parcels and passengers' luggage. The rear of the vehicle was modified by the addition of a platform which enabled passengers to join and alight at stations. There were also steps from this platform down to rail level. On some GNR lines railbuses stopped at level crossings where there were no platforms, and passengers could use these steps to enter and exit the vehicle, though this facility does not seem to have been used by the SL&NCR. The only drawback with the railbus was that it could only be driven from one end and had to be turned at the end of each journey, but as there were already turntables provided for the use of steam locomotives this was not a problem.

The immediate effect of the arrival of the first SL&NCR railbus was that it allowed the passenger service to be restored to the pre-strike level of three workings each way daily. In 1938 the original petrol engine was replaced by a Gardner diesel which delivered even greater economy. Such was the success of the first railbus, another was ordered from the GNR and delivered in the spring of 1938. Railbus A was scrapped following a collision with a steam locomotive at Glenfarne in March 1939 but several others followed and in 1947 when the company was still flush with the profits it had accumulated during the war a brand new railcar was ordered. This was built by Walker Brothers of Wigan who had been building articulated diesel-engined railcars for the County Donegal Railways since the 1930s. Railcar B as it was known was the only broad gauge Walker railcar to run in Ireland and was the pride of the line. It could seat 59 passengers and had a driving cab at each end so, unlike the railbuses, it did not have to be turned at the end of each journey.

When the line closed CIÉ bought the railcar and it remained in service with them until the 1970s. It was eventually passed to an abortive railway preservation scheme which was based at Mallow station but it was never restored and its condition worsened greatly with the passage of time. When the exhibits at Mallow were dispersed, Railcar B was given by Iarnród Éireann to the Downpatrick & County Down Railway which remains Ireland's only broad gauge heritage line. Though this historic vehicle was inherited by the D&CDR in an appalling state it is intended to restore it to running order. When funds and other resources permit Railcar B will be returned to her former glory, and a bit of SL&NCR history will be revived as she is put to work again among the drumlins of County Down.

As I hope it will be apparent by now, the SL&NCR was a singular line in so many ways, a one-off, quirky, even a bit eccentric. In its early days it had struggled to maintain its independence and yet by 1948 it had become the last independent railway company in the British Isles. Everything else on both sides of the Irish Sea had by then been nationalised and it was sustained by annual handouts from those recidivist railwayphobes at Stormont. Its singularity extended to the types of locomotives it used in that the SL&NCR's steam fleet largely consisted of one type of tank engine built by one manufacturer which had been developed and improved over the decades as each new locomotive was introduced.

This is a book about railway lines rather than railway locomotives but it will do no harm to take a moment to explain something about how these beautiful beasts, the very essence of the romance of the railway, are described. Steam locomotives are basically of two types, tank engines and tender engines. A tender engine carries its coal and water supplies in a purpose built vehicle which is semi-permanently coupled behind the engine itself. A tank engine's water is contained in tanks on both sides of the boiler, in a saddle tank which straddles the boiler or, in the case of some small or very early engines known as well tanks, in a container between the wheels. Most tank engines have a bunker for coal at the rear of their driving cabs. The most important components of the steam locomotive are the boiler and the wheels. Boilers vary enormously according to their size and the steam pressure they are able to maintain, which determine the resulting power output. Wheel sizes also vary greatly. Smaller wheels generally deliver a greater tractive force and are best suited for slower speeds. Engines used predominantly for hauling goods trains, where pulling power rather than speed is of the essence, would be in this category. On the other hand, express passenger types have larger wheels, making fewer revolutions, and are designed to run at much higher speeds. What made the SL&NCR tanks unusual was their wheel arrangement. This is usually described using the Whyte notation, a formula devised by an American engineer at the start of the last century which identifies the leading, coupled and trailing wheels in separate groups, with a zero included where no leading or trailing wheels are provided. This leads to hieroglyphics appearing in railway books such as 4-6-0, 2-6-4T (the 'T' denoting a tank engine) or in the case of our SL&NCR locos 0-6-4Ts.

The 0-6-4T wheel arrangement was a very unusual and infrequently used variation but it seemed to suit the SL&NCR. The first two of these were delivered in 1882 and were named, appropriately, *Fermanagh* and *Leitrim*. Three more followed by the turn of the century, *Lurganboy* in 1895 and *Lissadell* and *Hazlewood* in 1899, all named after the estates of directors or prominent backers of the company. These and the engines which followed were constructed by Beyer Peacock in Manchester, part of the total of 319 machines supplied by that firm to the Irish railway companies throughout the age of steam, a figure only bettered by Inchicore works in Dublin which built 358 locomotives. Whereas 99.9 per cent of railways around the world gave their locomotives numbers, the SL&NCR never did; they were known by their names only. There is something unutterably charming about this practice, as far removed as it is possible to go from today's world dominated by accountants and bean counters. We all romanticise and anthropomorphise the steam locomotive in one way or another. Even today children wave at steam trains while ignoring diesels and electrics, and yet to see this as part of the everyday culture and behaviour of a railway company tells us that this was much more than just a business or a means of getting passengers or cattle from A to B. It was a close knit and intimate community where sons followed fathers into the service of the company and generations of the same family were raised in the cottages provided beside the line's many level crossings to accommodate their custodians. And let us not forget that the personal pronoun applied to steam locomotives is *always* the feminine form. These were fine ladies, loved and respected and yet sometimes probably cursed by their men.

At different times other types of locomotives were tried, usually 0-6-0s or 4-4-0s, hired or bought second hand from the GNR, but when it came to buying new engines the order always went to Beyer Peacock and it was always for 0-6-4 tanks. With each infrequent order the basic design was developed and improved. The first arrivals in the twentieth century were *Sir Henry*, delivered in 1904 and named after the company's chairman Sir Henry Gore-Booth, and *Enniskillen* in 1905. These looked more modern and purposeful than the earlier trio. They had bigger boilers and were more powerful and did not have some of the ornate decorative flourishes of the first 0-6-4Ts. Known as the 'large tanks', the earlier engines inevitably now became the 'small tanks'. A further 'large tank' arrived in 1917 and was named *Lough Gill*. After that, nothing happened until 1951.

Two new 0-6-4Ts were ordered from Beyer Peacock when the company was still basking in its brief wartime flirtation with prosperity and were ready in 1949. However, in the interval between the order being placed and the time Beyer Peacock had completed the locomotives, normal service, in a financial sense, had been restored and the company found it could not afford to buy the engines. Negotiations began with the Northern Ireland government for a loan to pay for the locos and these dragged on into 1950 when a sort of hire purchase agreement was concluded with Beyer Peacock that allowed the new 0-6-4Ts, *Lough Melvin* and *Lough Erne*, to be finally delivered to the railway in the summer of 1951 though they carried plates on their bunkers asserting that they were the property of Beyer Peacock! The pair turned out to be the last conventional steam locomotives supplied to an Irish railway company.

Though it is now over 50 years since the SL&NCR closed and the passing years have taken its toll of those who had the chance to travel on it, many lovers of railways were drawn to this charming and endangered species, the independent railway, in the 1950s and their recollections and their photographs enable a journey along the line to be recreated. So let us enter the time machine and set the dials for Enniskillen station on a summer's evening in June 1951 and we will take a trip on the legendary 7.20pm mixed train to Sligo which was the only steam-hauled passenger service on the line by that time. The train conveyed both goods wagons and a coach for passengers which was always one of the trio of tricomposites built by Hurst Neilson at Motherwell in Scotland in 1924 to replace the carriages destroyed during the Civil War. It was called a tricomposite because it accommodated all three classes of passengers, 1st, 2nd and 3rd, in different compartments. However, as there was only one 1st class compartment and in order to provide an area for both smokers and non-smokers, this was divided down the middle by a wooden partition to keep everyone happy.

This was primarily a goods train and if there was not enough traffic to justify this second westbound goods working of the day, a railbus would run instead. But we are in luck this evening and as we walk towards the SL&NCR bay platform we see our tricomposite coupled behind an engine in the distance. The steam passenger service only operated in one direction, so earlier that day the coach which we will soon be boarding would have been worked back empty from Sligo in a goods train. Let us imagine that our engine is *Lough Melvin*, her new black paintwork shining in the evening sun which also highlights the plate on her bunker reminding us that she is still the property of Beyer Peacock. The rest of the train consists of a mixture of goods and cattle wagons with the guard's brake van bringing up the rear.

Heading west from the station which the SL&NCR shared with the GNR, we curve sharply to the right before the line takes us through an avenue of trees, part of the Castlecoole estate. Then we come to the major engineering feature on the route, Killyhevlin viaduct also known as Weir's bridge, a 467 ft girder bridge which carries the line over the River Erne. We get a wave from the gatekeeper at Lisgoole level crossing, the first of 28 sets of gates which were dotted along the line between Enniskillen and Collooney and after about 15 minutes we arrive at Florencecourt station 5¼ miles from Enniskillen at around 7.35pm. There is no passing loop here, just a siding and a goods store and indeed there is no village either. The station was named after the residence, some three miles distant to the south, of the Earl of Enniskillen who was one of the promoters of the line.

Leaving Florencecourt we soon pass through the halt at Abohill before reaching Belcoo & Blacklion, 12 miles from Enniskillen, where His Majesty's Customs inspect us and the train. This ritual humiliation of passengers went on at border stations every day for decades. It is hard to believe that the value of any contraband carried by the country men and women who constituted the majority of the passengers merited all this effort. I wonder if the excise men felt good as they went home after a shift; did they have a smile of smug satisfaction on their faces after they had confiscated a few pounds of butter or a couple of packets of tobacco from someone who could ill afford the loss? Three cheers for the EU for banishing such parasites from borders across the continent and reducing, in economic terms at least if not in the minds of a few fanatics, this great fault line across Ireland to no more than a squiggle on a map.

The dose was repeated at Glenfarne, the next station, where Irish customs did their work, as pointless and disruptive as that of their northern counterparts, reinforcing the division which the state that employed them was supposed to reject. Both Belcoo and Glenfarne stations are still in existence and have been beautifully restored. Belcoo retains its platform, station building, name board, goods store, signal box and level crossing gates. Only the tracks of the main line and the passing loop are missing. At Glenfarne the main station building has been extended with a new wing built at right angles to the original. However, this has been constructed with such care, using stonework and bargeboards which replicate those on the original building, that the job could have been done by the SL&NCR engineer himself. The goods store has been converted into a residence and the signal box also still exists though it is in need of restoration. There are railway style notice boards on the station building facing the platform and the corrugated iron shed where the Customs officers lurked between trains is probably in better condition now than it was in its heyday.

We have passed through a bit of County Cavan on the way between Belcoo and Glenfarne but there were no stations in that county, only a couple of level crossings. From Annagh crossing a mile or so before Glenfarne the line begins to climb for about 4 miles, much of it on gradients as steep as 1 in 50 towards its summit at Kilmakerrill. By now it is around 8.15pm and *Lough Melvin* has to work hard to start her train from the stop at Glenfarne and take it up the bank. It was a goods train making the descent from the summit with too much vigour to stop in time at the station which put an end to the career of the SL&NCR's first railbus in 1939.

Once Kilmakerrill summit, 367 ft above sea level, is breasted we pass through Kilmakerrill Halt which was opened in 1929 and then it is downhill all the way to Manorhamilton, though sharp reverse curves on the descent mean that the driver of *Lough Melvin* has to moderate his speed. Manorhamilton, just short of 25 miles from Enniskillen, is the nerve centre of the SL&NCR and we enter the station over a level crossing on the Enniskillen to Sligo road. The station was about half a mile from the centre of the town. Many British and Irish country stations were situated a long way from the places they were supposed to serve and in this respect Manorhamilton was not the worst offender. When the railway was the only means of transport apart from the horse and cart the location of stations would not have caused the railway builders too much concern as passengers and goods had no alternative but to come to them. However, once the internal combustion engine came on the scene, this became a serious deterrent to using the railways in many places. The company's workshops were at Manorhamilton. All locomotive repairs and maintenance were carried out in the two road stone-built shed at the Sligo end of the station. Only major work on boilers and fireboxes could not be tackled and had to be passed over to the Dundalk works of the GNR. All repairs to the railway's wagons and carriages were also done here in a separate shed.

Manorhamilton was one of those unlikely places dotted around Ireland where the opening of independent railways had created a little oasis full of the arcane engineering know-how which was required to keep steam locomotives and the stock they pulled in more or less good order. Tralee, Ennis, Augher in County Tyrone and Ballinamore, also in County Leitrim, are some of the other places where railway workshops were to be found. The men who worked there had to be masters of many trades and they had nothing like the facilities which were to be found at the works of the big companies, such as Dundalk and Inchicore. When these railways closed, or the work was moved to the major works because of amalgamations or rationalisation, this expertise was also dispersed.

Apart from the workshops, Manorhamilton had a passing loop, goods shed and sidings and also a carriage shed, and from the train we catch a glimpse of a couple of the SL&NCR's buses in the station yard. The company began to operate bus services in April 1945 and between then and 1957 a total of nine buses were acquired though only four were usually needed for normal timetabled services. Legislation in Northern Ireland barred railway companies from operating bus services but no such impediment was in force south of the border so all the SL&NCR's bus services operated in the Free State/Irish Republic. The main route was that from Blacklion to Sligo via Manorhamilton and Glencar which had one or two services six days a week. Other routes served remote villages such as Ballinaglera, Dowra and Bohy, but these usually only ran on some weekdays. In these days when politicians and transport analysts frequently urge the creation of integrated transport networks it is salutary to remember that this was exactly what the SL&NCR on a small scale and the GNR on a much larger one were offering in the Irish Republic in the post-war era. Today, Manorhamilton is still recognisable as a former railway station. From the road the station forecourt has the look of railway premises, and the corrugated iron hut at right angles to the public road and the stone wall which runs from it to the main building is not much different from a view of the same location taken before the Second World War. The goods shed still exists, and the last time I passed by there was even a bus in the station yard, though not one of the little Bedfords in two-tone green livery favoured by the old company.

Leaving Manorhamilton at 8.50pm, as it is midsummer the light is still good by the time we reach Dromahair 8½ miles distant at around 9.15pm. We pass the site of Lisgorman Halt, now closed, before coming to the one level crossing (Cleen, No 18 crossing) on this section. Dromahair, which had a signal box but no passing loop, was about a mile outside the village and was the only two-storey station building on the line. This has been carefully converted into a private residence, accessed by a gap in a wall where there was a level crossing over the road at the Sligo end of the station. The goods shed behind the station and roughly parallel to it is also still there but it is disappearing under ivy and other vegetation. After leaving the station the train passes through another avenue of trees on the way to Ballintogher, three miles on and after another three miles the final halt, Ballygawley, is reached. For a change this is convenient to the habitation it served. Our steam service only called at the halts still open, Abohill, Kilmackerrell, Ballintogher and Ballygawley, on request.

It is getting dark when we reach Collooney, 41½ miles from Enniskillen at 9.45pm. We can hear cattle lowing in their pens. This time tomorrow night many of them will be on ships bound for England. Collooney has two platforms which can just about be made out today under a blanket of vegetation. Nothing else remains of the SL&NCR station apart from these overgrown remains. Just beyond the bridge over the Owenmore River at the western end of the station the connection to the erstwhile WL&W line, the southern siding, diverges. This has seen little use since for many years and latterly it has been used to store wagons.

Leaving Collooney there is less than a mile of the SL&NCR proper to travel on before we reach the site of Carrignagat Junction where the line from Enniskillen joined the MGWR route from Dublin to Sligo. The original signal box was destroyed during the Civil War and was replaced by a temporary structure in use until 1930 when the GSR abolished the junction here altogether. From then on two separate parallel single lines ran for about a mile from the site of the junction to Ballysodare station where the physical connection between the Dublin and Enniskillen lines was now made. We leave our last stop at Ballysodare at 9.55pm and it takes another 10 minutes to cover the remaining 4½ miles into Sligo. Here the wagons will be shunted and some will be taken down the branch to Sligo Quay. *Lough Melvin* and the coach will be stabled and if there are enough goods wagons at Enniskillen to justify the trip, the 7.20pm will set out again on the same journey tomorrow evening.

The story of the 1957 closures has been dealt with in the last chapter. This is that sorry tale from the SL&NCR perspective. The outlook for the railway was not good in the years following the Second World War. With the easing of the wartime fuel shortages, traffic began to drift back on to the roads and in 1946 the government of Northern Ireland cut back its subsidy to £1,500 per year. There was some increase in payments from the GNR for through traffic emanating from the SL&NCR which at first offset this, but by 1951 the once mighty GNR itself was in trouble and was taken over by both governments in 1953 and run by a new body, the Great Northern Railway Board, on which sat representatives from the two jurisdictions. The SL&NCR was by now operating at a substantial annual loss. In 1955 it was just over £10,000, and the southern government got involved in providing subsidies, while Stormont was somehow persuaded to double its Grant-In-Aid to £3,000 annually. In 1955 the northern government announced that it would no longer provide funding for the line and it looked for a time as if the SL&NCR would at last succumb. However, Dublin increased its payments in the face of lobbying from the cattle traders for whom the line was still a vital link and the immediate crisis was averted.

By 1956 it was becoming clear that the Stormont government was determined to close the GNR cross-border lines and was simply prepared to ignore the storm of criticism that this was generating. This sealed the fate of the SL&NCR. With no outlet for its traffic at Enniskillen, it had no option but to announce that it would be closing down on the same day of infamy which saw the closure of the GNR lines through Enniskillen. Technically, this was the reason the line closed. The southern government only announced it would withdraw its subsidy to the SL&NCR when it became clear that the lines beyond Enniskillen were to be closed. Collateral damage indeed. How much longer a charming anachronism like the SL&NCR could have survived is difficult to assess but as late as 1956 the West of Ireland Cattle Traders Association were prepared to pay a levy on each wagon of cattle forwarded over the line to help keep it open.

The Sligo, Leitrim & Northern Counties began its operations in 1879 and was forced to shut up shop in 1957. Its trains thus ran for a period of 78 years. Had it been promoted a few years later, it would almost certainly have benefited from baronial guarantees at least and its first two decades might have been spared the financial turbulence which surrounded it. When its financial situation was finally stabilised in the late 1890s, it proved to be a viable operation within the modest parameters that could be applied to other small Irish railway companies. While it was far from a roaring success in fiscal terms, neither was it a lost cause. Receipts comfortably exceeded expenditure and while there was never a great deal of money left to invest in its rolling stock and infrastructure there was sufficient to expand the wagon fleet to meet with increasing traffic levels and occasionally to pay for new locomotives. The railway found a niche for itself in serving the livestock trade which was an important component in the economy of the districts through which it ran and those of the adjoining counties, on both sides of the border. Even when the balance sheet began to swing into the red in the 1930s, the SL&NCR was too important to be allowed to go under and the subsidies, no doubt handed over with ill grace by the government of Northern Ireland, is evidence of this.

Throughout its history, the SL&NCR benefited from its close relationship with the GNR which almost acted as its patron. In turn the larger company derived substantial revenues from the volume of goods and especially cattle traffic which was taken forward from Enniskillen in GNR goods trains each working day. The GNR supplied second-hand locomotives at times and of course built the railbuses which allowed the SL&NCR to maintain a passenger service at a fraction of the cost of using steam locomotives for the work. It is ironic that it was the emasculation of its benign and helpful neighbour which finally sealed the fate of the SL&NCR. Once the closure of the GNR lines beyond Enniskillen was imposed, there was nowhere for its cattle traffic to go except on to the hopelessly inadequate roads of the border counties, and the railway had no option but to shut down its operations.

Today much of the trackbed survives as do several of the stations and many former gatehouses; the trackbed which SL&NCR trains used on the last leg of their journeys from the site of Carrignagat Junction into Sligo sees the passage of Iarnród Éireann trains on the Dublin to Sligo service, and there is a possibility that the line from Claremorris may be revived making

Collooney a junction once again. The branch to Sligo Quay, used by SL&NCR goods trains, closed only in recent years as IÉ rushed recklessly to get itself out of the freight business, but there is almost nothing left at Enniskillen to remind us that this was once a major railway centre served by two separate companies.

As noted above, Railcar B survives in the care of the preservationists at Downpatrick, as does one of the last pair of locomotives delivered to the railway in 1951. This is not the engine which hauled our virtual 7.20pm mixed, *Lough Melvin*, but the other one, *Lough Erne*. When the line closed both engines were still the subject of the hire purchase deal done with Beyer Peacock in 1951 and in 1959 they were bought by the Ulster Transport Authority. Though they retained their names they were given the numbers 26 and 27 and used for shunting at goods yards in the Belfast area. With the demise of the UTA both locomotives passed into the hands of Northern Ireland Railways in 1968 though in that year No 26 *Lough Melvin* was withdrawn.

No 27 *Lough Erne* remained in service until 1970, almost to the very end of steam working in Ireland the following year. It was saved from the scrapmen and has been entrusted to the care of the Railway Preservation Society of Ireland ever since. The locomotive has never been restored by the RPSI for reasons which are understandable enough. The Society has now been running steam specials all over Ireland for more than 40 years, but it has had to focus its scarce human and financial resources on locomotives which can haul these trains at reasonable speeds without having to make too many stops for coal and water so as not to interfere with the regular revenue earning timetabled services run by NIR and IÉ. *Lough Erne*'s limited coal and water capacity does not make her an ideal candidate for such work and has meant that she has had to stay in the shadows. At least she is safe and in good hands and, given some of the miracles that railway preservationists have wrought over the years, she may yet come into the limelight at some time in the future, perhaps renewing her old acquaintance with Railcar B. If this reunion of old friends ever comes about it will not take place beside the lakes and rivers and the rushy fields of those border counties which once was their home.

Chapter 4 ❧

THE PREMIER LINE IN COUNTY LOUTH

No one could accuse Victorian railway companies on either side of the Irish Sea of reticence or self-deprecation. Many of the embryonic schemes of the 1830s had used the word 'Grand' in their titles, though by the 1840s this had largely been supplanted by the use of the rather more assertive adjective 'Great', which was used in the names of most of the bigger companies irrespective as to whether their performance actually merited this moniker. There was however one major British railway company which stood out from the pack almost because it had not described itself as great. That company probably felt the use of the word 'Great' was understating its importance. It preferred to refer to itself simply as 'the Premier Line'. This chapter tells the story of how this great monolith, the London & North Western Railway, based at Euston station in the heart of London, created a little replica of itself on the other side of the Irish Sea in the unlikely setting of the environs of Greenore, on the shores of Carlingford Lough, in County Louth.

The L&NWR was formed in 1846 with the merger of the London & Birmingham, the Manchester & Birmingham and the Grand Junction Railways. The previous year the GJR had taken over the Liverpool & Manchester of Stephenson's *Rocket* fame, the world's first inter-city railway. Therefore the newly formed L&NWR already served London, Birmingham, Manchester and Liverpool. In time its trains would also reach Leeds and Carlisle and in co-operation with Scottish companies would serve Glasgow and Edinburgh. It principal route was that along the West Coast to Scotland and as the nineteenth century progressed many secondary and branch lines were added to its network. At the height of its pomp just before the Great War it operated a total route mileage of more than 1,500, almost half that of the entire national network in Ireland. The L&NWR employed in excess of 100,000 staff and was for decades recognised as the largest joint stock company in the world. Its locomotive works at Crewe in Cheshire was probably the biggest railway owned works on the planet, employing over 20,000 people at its peak. Between 1843 and the end of steam locomotive building in the 1950s Crewe turned out over 7,000 engines.

From its earliest days the L&NWR took a keen interest in trade with Ireland on the shipping routes across the Irish Sea. The GJR had taken over the Chester & Crewe Railway in 1840 but this was merely to be the overture to a much bigger project, the Chester & Holyhead Railway. Since the Act of Union of 1800 the importance of getting mail and government papers quickly and safely between London and Dublin was a high priority for the British government. The shortest sea route to Dublin was that from Holyhead on the west coast of Anglesey, but to get to Holyhead meant a sometimes treacherous journey through the mountains of north Wales. In 1811 the Scottish engineer Thomas Telford was asked to survey a new road from London to Holyhead to expedite the Irish mails. The first section from London to Shrewsbury was relatively straightforward and followed the course of Watling Street, a road first built by the Romans. However, west of Shrewsbury the 106 miles to Holyhead presented many engineering challenges, none more so than bridging the Menai Straits between the mainland and Anglesey. Telford's elegant solution to this problem, a suspension bridge high enough to allow the tall masts of sailing ships to pass underneath at the insistence of the Admiralty, is still in use today.

When the Holyhead Road was finally fully opened in 1836,

though the journey time for a mail coach was reduced by 12 hours, it still took over a day to make the journey from London to Holyhead. Ironically in 1839, just a few years after Telford's great project was completed, the previously unheard of speed offered by the new railways led to the Irish mails being transferred from Holyhead to Liverpool which from 1838 had a rail connection to London. Using the railway and steam ships from Liverpool meant that the mails could now reach Dublin in 22 hours if all went according to plan. Whilst this was quicker than Telford's road, the disadvantage of using Liverpool rather than Holyhead was the much longer sea journey.

The quickest solution of all was to build a railway to Holyhead combining the speed of the railways with a shorter sea crossing, so it is not surprising that an Act to enable this to happen was passed by parliament in July 1844. The Chester & Holyhead Railway was authorised to raise over £2 million to build its 85 mile long double track main line. The first sod was ceremonially cut at Conwy in March 1845 and within a year over 5,000 navvies, many of them Irish, were employed building the line. Parliament had given the company permission to breach the historic walls of both Chester and Conwy and the line's engineer Robert Stephenson developed a new type of tubular bridge to cross the estuary at Conwy and the Menai Straits. The Britannia bridge over the Straits, like Telford's before it, had to be at a great height to enable shipping to pass underneath unimpeded. The first 60 miles to Bangor were opened in 1848 with trains going through to Holyhead from March 1850. With the opening of the railway to Bangor came the first running, on 1 August 1848, of what was probably the earliest named train in the world, *The Irish Mail*. This was the precursor to the *Orient Express*, the *City of New Orleans*, the *Flying Scotsman*, even our own dear *Enterprise* and a legion of other named trains across the globe, adding a new level of romance to an already romantic form of travel. The journey from Euston to Holyhead was 264 miles by rail.

The mail steamers themselves had traditionally been operated by the Admiralty but in 1850, in an early example of privatisation, the contract was put out to tender and awarded to the City of Dublin Steam Packet Company, much to the disgust of the Chester & Holyhead and their allies at Euston who expected to get it after going to the trouble of building their new railway. With the mail contract came the prestigious initials RMS standing for Royal Mail Ship which preceded the names of the vessels themselves. The CofDSPCo continued to hang on to the contract for most of the nineteenth century, and this must have been particularly galling to the L&NWR which formally took over the C&H in 1859. Though deprived of the mail contract, the L&NWR began to develop its own shipping services across the Irish Sea, focusing on the port of Dublin rather than Kingstown which it finally abandoned in 1861, leaving that route the sole preserve of the CofDSPCo. The first L&NWR steamers ran from Holyhead to the North Wall in Dublin in 1848. They carried passengers, goods and livestock, but only for a very short and turbulent period towards the end of the nineteenth century did they convey the Irish mails.

The L&NWR encouraged the other railways to extend their lines to the North Wall. The first to get there was the Midland Great Western's Liffey branch, the line which still runs beside the Royal Canal at the back of Croke Park. This opened from Liffey Junction in Phibsboro to the North Wall in 1864. The Midland's long-time rival, the Great Southern & Western, next opened a line from Islandbridge Junction just outside Kingsbridge station which tunnelled under the Phoenix Park to join the Midland's Liffey branch at Glasnevin Junction. The L&NWR contributed £70,000 to the cost of the GS&WR line which would give traffic from that railway's great network of lines a direct route to the L&NWR's steamers at the North Wall. In conjunction with this, the L&NWR opened in 1877 a hotel and a new station across the road from where its ships berthed. Their first railway venture on Irish soil was less than half a mile in length, connecting its new station, goods and cattle yards to a GS&WR line at Church Road

Junction which in turn was connected to the Liffey branch. The same year a connection to the GNR at East Wall Junction was opened and from then until 1921 regular passenger services were operated to the L&NWR's North Wall station, providing connections to their steamers.

The hubris of The Premier Line may have been driven by that lack of the mail contract but the company seemed to be determined to get its hands on as much of the Irish Sea traffic as possible and to do this it looked beyond its existing route from Holyhead to Dublin. In 1870, jointly with the Lancashire & Yorkshire Railway, the L&NWR began to run steamers from Fleetwood to Belfast and Derry. Further north in 1872, the L&NWR began running through trains from Euston to Stranraer in the far south-west of Scotland promoting this as the 'short sea route', which it was, though the rail journey from the capital was far from short. Predating all of these developments the L&NWR spotted another opportunity to extend its dominance of the Irish Sea traffic. In the 1860s there was no regular service out of any port between Belfast and Dublin and it was to fill that gap that the gaze of those in charge at Euston began to focus on Greenore in County Louth.

Greenore stood at the southern end of Carlingford Lough and was almost equidistant from Newry and Dundalk, both ports in their own rights but with problems associated with their operation. Newry could only be reached by a ship canal and access to the port of Dundalk was subject to the state of the tide. Greenore was a natural deep-water harbour waiting to be developed. In the early 1860s the two railway companies closest to Greenore began to examine possible railway connections. The Newry & Armagh surveyed a line down the shore of Carlingford Lough while the Dundalk & Enniskillen almost from the outset sought the support of the L&NWR not just to build a railway from Dundalk to Greenore but to create a new Irish Sea route by developing the port and drawing passenger and livestock traffic from across the north-west of Ireland to it. In 1862 the D&E

changed its name to the Irish North Western Railway to reflect that its interests now extended beyond the two towns in its original title but also to impress the L&NWR which it was busily wooing for support. James Barton, the INWR's engineer, conducted extensive surveys not just of the railway routes to Greenore but of the channels and approaches to the port itself. Barton's plans and estimates were passed to Euston where there was great enthusiasm for the scheme. The L&NWR directors indicated their full support in 1863. In a report to their shareholders they wrote, 'The Directors, therefore, have concurred with the Irish North Western Company in arrangements by which, without any outlay of capital by this company, an extension of that line will be secured from Dundalk to Greenore Point.' As things were to turn out this was to be a major miscalculation. The scheme was to cost The Premier Line a small fortune.

The Irish promoters of the two companies which were planning to build lines to Greenore—the Newry & Greenore and the Dundalk & Greenore—presented their schemes before parliament in 1863 and both were successful in obtaining their respective Acts. The port and its facilities were to be jointly developed. Each company needed over £100,000 and a familiar quadrille was now performed as they both sought to raise the money, with little apparent success. Their efforts were hampered by the economic crisis of 1866 caused by the failure of the London bankers Overend and Guerney. The delay was fortuitous in one way in that it allowed Barton to complete his work on the port itself. While the involvement of the L&NWR with the D&G became more obvious, with some D&G board meetings now being held at Euston, the other company, the N&G, languished and even though it returned to parliament to have the time allowed to complete the line extended and to seek powers to raise more capital, no construction work was undertaken. The company collapsed in 1867 when it was unable to honour some of the financial commitments it had made earlier in connection with expenditure on the port.

The D&G obtained a new Act in 1867 which allowed it to take over the port and brought increased L&NWR involvement with provision for a subscription of up to £130,000 from the English company. This signalled the effective takeover of the whole scheme by the L&NWR. In 1868 the chairman and secretary of the L&NWR assumed those roles with the D&G and the company's head office was moved to Euston. A contract was finally placed and construction of the line from Dundalk to Greenore at last got under way. When the INWR pleaded that it did not have the funds to provide locomotives and rolling stock for the new line, the L&NWR provided its own, based on contemporary Crewe designs of the period which were supplied in L&NWR livery.

The line from Dundalk and the new port were opened with great ceremony by Earl Spencer, the Lord Lieutenant of Ireland, on 30 April 1873 and no expense was spared to make the accompanying junket a memorable one. A total of 800 guests arrived on four special trains and two steamers. After the speeches the invited guests retired to a banquet, prepared by a caterer brought in from Dublin. This was served in what was to be the goods shed at Greenore suitably titivated for the occasion. Passenger sailings began on 1 May and it was possible to leave Euston at 5.15pm and arrive in Greenore via Holyhead at 7.15am the next morning. In addition to the fast trains connecting with the steamers there were three local services daily between Dundalk and Greenore serving intermediate stations. The main drawback with the new line was the arrangements at Dundalk. The D&G had its own station at Quay Street in Dundalk and just beyond this the line made an end-on junction with the INWR at Barrack Street. Trains from Greenore then crossed over the Dublin to Belfast line on the level at Dundalk Square Crossing before reversing at Dundalk West Cabin to reach the town's main station. These manoeuvres meant that it could take a train from Greenore up to 15 minutes to complete the last two miles of its journey.

Once the line to Dundalk was open, thoughts turned to the other part of the original scheme, the connection from Greenore to Newry. A new Act was obtained in 1873 which changed the name of the company to the Dundalk, Newry & Greenore and provided authority to build a line 13 miles in length from Greenore via Omeath to a junction in Newry with the existing Newry & Armagh company's line and the use of its Edward Street station in the town. The 1873 Act increased the capital of the DN&G to £400,000 of which £325,000 was provided by the L&NWR. More and more money was poured into the company by the L&NWR until eventually its investment was in the region of £600,000. This was a very different story to that given by the L&NWR directors in the report to their shareholders back in 1863. The line to Newry opened in August 1876 to a newly built DN&G station at Bridge Street. Trains were not extended to Edward Street station until 1880 when the connecting line from Bridge Street to what was now the Great Northern Railway's station was opened.

A railway that had begun life as an extension to the INWR was now effectively a wholly owned subsidiary of the English company. Greenore became an L&NWR town. The two main roads in the village were called Euston Street and Angelsey Terrace and some of the stone and other materials used to build them was imported from north Wales. The Welsh connection did not end there. The day-to-day management of the various functions of the railway was delegated to the L&NWR official closest on the other side of the Irish Sea. Thus at one time the L&NWR District Engineer in Bangor (the Welsh one) was responsible for the maintenance of the track and structures of the line, and its locomotives and rolling stock were under the control of an engineer based at Crewe. There had been nothing of any significance at Greenore before the railway arrived but now it became a hub of maritime and railway activity. A whole new community was established, based around the port and the railway. In addition to the houses the company built for its workers—there were graduations in the size of these depending on the status of the occupant—the L&NWR provided other amenities such as a police station, a school, a house for the schoolmaster and a shop.

The facilities provided at the port itself were state of the art, 1870s style. A substantial terminus with an overall roof was built at the quayside. In terms of its appearance the station was not unlike that at Holyhead, though built to a smaller scale. Its interior design was pure L&NWR. All its fixtures and fittings such as platform barrows, station seats, noticeboards and signage were to the company's standard designs. The platform was linked to the ships by an early type of escalator designed, by the company's engineer James Barton, to move crowds of passengers quickly from train to ship, under cover all the way. The escalator passed through a subway under the goods lines on the quayside, keeping passengers clear of the hazard that might have been caused if they had to cross these tracks to reach the ships. On the quayside itself there were hydraulically operated gangways providing access to the ships which could be adjusted to compensate for the state of the tide. All of this made for speedy and convenient interchange between train and ship, with as little as 15 minutes being allowed for transfer from one mode of transport to the other.

The company opened a hotel a short distance from the station, again designed by Barton and built in red brick. This was extended in the 1890s to provide a total of 42 bedrooms. Several bungalows which could be hired by visitors were also built. In the hotel every plate and piece of cutlery would have carried the L&NWR's monogram or initials and contemporary accounts speak of the sumptuous style in which the public rooms were fitted out. Hot and cold fresh and sea water baths were provided. There were extensive gardens and tennis courts for the guests and, in an effort to encourage tourists to visit Greenore, the L&NWR opened a twelve-hole golf course there in 1896 which was later extended to the full eighteen holes.

The corporate identity was not confined to the buildings at the port. It extended into other aspects of the railway and its operations, notably the signals which were of the L&NWR pattern and the rolling stock all of which was supplied by the company. The original intention was that the INWR would work the line but as its role was marginalised, largely through the company's traditionally parlous financial state, the L&NWR took over the provision of the locomotives, wagons and carriages that would work the line, as well as everything else. From the beginning services on the Dundalk line were operated by locomotives built at Crewe and carriages made at the L&NWR's carriage works at Wolverton in Buckinghamshire. For the opening of the line from Dundalk to Greenore in 1873 three 0-6-0 saddle tank locomotives were built at Crewe. These machines were very similar to a type of engine called Special Tanks which were being turned out for use in England at the time. They were designed by John Ramsbottom who had been the company's locomotive engineer since the 1850s and were based on his most successful and prolific design, the DX six coupled goods engines. Between 1858 and 1872 a total of 943 of these machines had been built, an early example of standardisation on a massive scale.

The Greenore engines were very similar, both mechanically and visually, to their counterparts across the Irish Sea. They displayed many contemporary L&NWR design details such as their cast number plates and the standard design of chimneys and safety valves. As built they offered virtually no protection from the weather but were later given proper cabs. Their counterparts across the Irish Sea were often used for shunting in goods yards where the lack of cabs, whilst making life uncomfortable for their crews in inclement weather, was probably just about tolerable. In Ireland, however, they were used on a line which was over 12 miles in length and ran close to the coast. Working on the railway in almost any capacity in the nineteenth century whilst offering secure employment involved long hours, few if any paid holidays and low pay. In this respect the railways were no worse than other industries but with the perspective of time it is hard not to reflect unfavourably on the contempt which Victorian capitalists had for those who made them rich. Two further locomotives were supplied in 1876 for the opening of the line to Newry and a final saddle tank was sent over to Ireland in 1898.

After all the money which the L&NWR had spent on opening the two railways, in developing Greenore as a port, building a hotel and a village for its workers, the company found it had one major problem on its hands. Despite its huge investment, the financial returns from the whole enterprise were desperately disappointing. Receipts from both the railway and the steamers were poor from the outset and matters did not improve. In 1893 a new L&NWR General Manager conducted an investigation into the route and found the company suffered losses of £28,000 that year, with the railways not even generating enough revenue to cover their operating costs. The reasons for this are not hard to deduce. The major flows of traffic from the north-west which had been anticipated when the project had first been mooted proved to be illusory. In addition, the service that was provided via Greenore was poor. In every instance it was quicker for travellers from London to Belfast or Londonderry to take a steamer to the North Wall in Dublin where they could join a connecting GNR train at the L&NWR's station there for a quick run north. The ships used on the Dublin service were also generally newer and quicker. In 1876, not long after the port of Greenore and its railways had opened, the company offered its quickest service from London to Ireland to date but this ran from Holyhead to Dublin, not Greenore.

Another factor mitigating against the success of the Greenore route came into play in 1883 when the government awarded the coveted contract to carry the Irish mails to the L&NWR. This led to uproar both in sections of the press in Ireland and from many Irish Nationalist MPs in the House of Commons who objected strongly to the contract being taken from an Irish concern, the City of Dublin Steam Packet Company, and awarded to an English railway. In the face of this concerted opposition the decision was reversed and the contract was restored to the CofDSPCo. The final triumph of the L&NWR came in 1920 when the contract was put out to tender again, with the railway company's bid being accepted. This turned out to be a pyrrhic victory, however, as partition was to diminish the importance of the mail contract and through passenger services to and from the L&NWR station at the North Wall ended in 1921.

The L&NWR did not seem to wake up to the problems with the Greenore route until the 1890s. Faced with continuing losses, the company responded by spending even more money on its Irish satellite. Track and signalling on the two railway lines were improved and it was at this time that the golf course was opened and attempts were made to develop Greenore as a tourist destination. New carriages were supplied including some Tricomposites running on bogies which were used on the boat trains to Belfast. More importantly three new ships were provided in 1897/98 and the connecting railway services were speeded up. The results of all this investment were that the railways began to show a small surplus of receipts over expenditure for the first time in the late 1890s. The route came closest to profit in the years before the First World War. In 1906 a passenger could leave Euston at 7.30pm and arrive in Holyhead at 1.15am. The steamer departed 25 minutes later, arriving at Greenore at 6.00am. The connecting boat train for Belfast left at 6.15am and arrived in the city at 7.40am, the whole journey taking just a shade over 12 hours. Passengers going in the other direction left Belfast at 7.00pm, arriving in Euston at 7.30am the next morning. At this time there was also a through carriage for Derry which was detached from the Belfast train at Portadown and arrived at the GNR station at Foyle Road in the Maiden City at 10.05am. The connection from Derry in the other direction left at 5.15pm.

The only significant accident in the history of the two railways occurred in June 1904 and involved a special train which had originated on the Sligo, Leitrim & Northern Counties Railway, carrying migrant workers to England to work on the harvest. This was 15 years after the Armagh disaster, the worst accident ever to occur on an Irish railway when inadequate brakes had caused a packed excursion train to roll out of control down an incline, to be wrecked when it hit another train coming towards the runaway carriages on the single line. On this occasion, the brakes of the DN&G engine which took over from a GNR locomotive at Quay Street station in Dundalk were incompatible with those on the SL&NCR coaches at the head of the train and it ran out of control on the descent from Bush station to Greenore. The train crashed through the buffer stops at the terminus and came to rest up against the wall of the refreshment room. Fortunately none of the passengers was seriously injured and they were able to continue their journey to England on the steamer later that evening.

This incident highlights how slow at least some of the Irish railway companies were to learn the lessons of the Armagh disaster and how weak was the regulatory regime which was supposed to enforce these lessons. Those SL&NCR coaches were still fitted with a type of braking system called Smith's non-automatic vacuum brake, the one which had been at least partly responsible for propelling 78 souls to their death on that incline outside Armagh in 1889. A far worse fate befell one of the Greenore steamers on 3 November 1916. The *Connemara* left Holyhead that night and headed out into the teeth of a strong south-westerly gale. She was about three miles out from Greenore when she collided with a collier, the *Retriever*, en route from Liverpool to Newry. The storm had extinguished the navigation lights on the *Retriever* and her crew had been unable to relight them because of the weather conditions that night. Both ships sank quickly. One member of the nine-man crew of the *Retriever* survived but all 86 passengers and crew on board the *Connemara* were lost.

A route which struggled to make a profit in the benign trading conditions before the Great War was particularly vulnerable in the changed world of the post-war era. The DN&G was affected by radical changes on both sides of the Irish Sea. Partition left the port and most of the railways in the Free State but the areas from which it drew much of its through traffic were now in Northern Ireland. The initial problems concerned the line to Dundalk which suffered many attacks from Irregulars during the Civil War. The worst of these caused considerable damage to Ballymascanlon viaduct in September 1922 which closed the Dundalk line for some time. The new border saw the establishment of Customs posts at Newry's Bridge Street station and Omeath.

Across the Irish Sea, the government sponsored the amalgamation of Britain's railways into four large companies in 1923. The L&NWR became part of the London, Midland & Scottish Railway. The LMS had inherited other Irish interests. Another of its constituents, the Midland Railway, owned the lines which radiated out from York Road station in Belfast, serving Larne, Londonderry and Portrush as well as many towns in mid-Ulster such as Magherafelt and Cookstown. The Midland also had a half share, with the GNR, in the County Donegal narrow gauge system. However, the Greenore lines were now in another jurisdiction. Anyone sending goods or livestock (the latter had become a mainstay of the traffic through the port) from locations which were now in Northern Ireland, had to go through the performance of paperwork at the border. In any case, the LMS had plenty of alternative shipping services from Northern Ireland to destinations in England and Scotland which could cater for much of the traffic that might have been routed through Greenore in previous times. Those other routes did not involve delays at the border.

The losses began to mount throughout the 1920s, that brief era of breaking even before the war becoming a distant memory. Passenger accommodation on the steamers was ended in 1925 and the service on the sea route was reduced to three sailings per week carrying goods and livestock only. The LMS found itself running loss-making railways in a foreign country. While there was a case to keep the lines open as feeder services for goods and livestock traffic destined for the remaining sailings, the company entered into prolonged negotiations with the GNR which eventually resulted in that company taking over the working and maintenance of both railway lines, and management of the hotel, in July 1933. Much of the original rolling stock was transferred to the Northern Counties section of the LMS in Northern Ireland, though the surviving five L&NWR saddle tanks (one was withdrawn in 1928) remained at work on the lines as did some of the six-wheeled carriages. These carriages were never repainted in GNR livery and continued to run in their L&NWR colours right through until their withdrawal. In an effort to cut operating costs the GNR introduced one of its railbuses on the Greenore lines in 1935. Additional halts were opened on the Dundalk line in the summer of 1935 at Crossaleney, Gyles Quay, Annaloughan and Bellurgan Point, and from the same period the railbuses stopped at two level crossings on the Newry line in an attempt to stimulate passenger traffic. The result of these changes was to reduce the losses but the lines never came anywhere close to making a profit.

The number of regular sailings using the port declined again during the Second World War. The trains were busier during this period, with a resurgence of passenger traffic because of draconian restrictions on the availability of petrol which drove most private motorists off the roads. While this propelled the other Irish railways briefly back into profit in the 1940s, the DN&G managed to buck the trend and still post losses of over £30,000 in 1945. Another major problem loomed in 1948 when the railways of Britain were nationalised by the post-war Labour government. The newly formed British Transport Commission, like the LMS before it, inherited a loss-making railway and an underused port, in another jurisdiction. The annual losses had risen by 1950 to the region of £50,000 per year. There was no post-war boom in traffic so the BTC came to the inevitable conclusion that the lines would have to close.

The last steamer left Greenore on 29 December 1951 and the last trains from Greenore to Newry and Dundalk ran on the 31st of that month. However, this was far from the end of the story. While the withdrawal of services was relatively straightforward, the formal winding up of the owning company and the disposal of its assets set in place a process of Byzantine complexity which was not concluded until 1957. All through the history of the line the DN&G company had remained in existence as a separate body with its own directors. It had never been formally amalgamated with the L&NWR or the LMS. It was a company set up under English law but operating mainly in another state. In addition it owned land and structures in what was now the Irish Republic and Northern Ireland. An order to abandon its assets in Northern Ireland was passed by the Stormont government in 1952 (they were good at this sort of thing), though it was not until 1956 that a similar process had been completed in the Republic. The final act was to dissolve the company itself and authority for this was given in a clause included in a bill presented by the BTC to the parliament at Westminster. On 26 July the DN&G board met for the last time, at Euston station as usual, five days later the BTC's bill received Royal Assent and finally the Dundalk, Newry & Greenore Railway Company officially and legally ceased to exist. All railway companies needed an Act of Parliament to allow them to commence their activities. I can think of no other which required one to put an end to them.

Just one piece of DN&G rolling stock survives—six wheel First/Second Composite carriage No 1 built at Wolverton by the L&NWR in 1909 which has been beautifully restored, gleaming in the L&NWR livery that it carried throughout its life, in the railway gallery at the Ulster Folk & Transport Museum at Cultra in County Down. Sadly none of the five original saddle tank engines which were still in existence when the line closed was preserved. Shortly after trains ceased running two of the major structures on the Dundalk line, the iron viaducts at Castletown and Ballymascanlon, were sold for scrap. However, there are still traces of the formation to be seen on this section, notably an overbridge and the station building at Bush. The formation of the line south from Newry ran beside the ship canal, and shortly after the railway closed Armagh County Council used parts of the trackbed to widen the road from Newry to Carlingford. At Omeath, the station platform and the house provided for the custodian of the adjacent level crossing are extant; there is a gap in the wall where the level crossing gates once stood. The attractive stone-built station building at Carlingford is in good condition and has found a new use as a tourist office.

There is much in Greenore itself to remind one of its origins. Euston Street and Angelsey Terrace survive more or less as built by the company in the 1870s. Euston Street is a particular little architectural gem. The golf club is still there, acquired by its members when the assets of the DN&G were disposed of in the 1950s. Sadly of the station itself there is little trace beyond a wall facing the quay and a couple of water tanks. However, perhaps the biggest disgrace was the destruction of the hotel as recently as 2006 in order to allow the owners of the port to build a warehouse on its site. It had admittedly been disused for many years and was in a poor state of repair but the refusal of Louth County Council to give the building protected status on the grounds that it had no architectural or historic value is almost unbelievable. The Council gave permission for its demolition in spite of submissions from bodies such as Dúchas—itself since demolished—and An Taisce recommending its preservation. So we have lost a fine and historic railway hotel, a symbol along with the station as to why there is anything at Greenore at all. But there is a grand warehouse there now and somebody is making a few shekels from it so everything is fine.

The logic of this is that commerce must supersede culture and heritage at every turn. So what price then a cracking new glass-and-steel shopping centre on the site of the Bank of Ireland in Dame Street or maybe a nice big new hotel, let's call it Christchurch Towers—you can imagine where that would be located! I suspect that many of us had hoped that this vision for the future development of Ireland had been consigned to the history books, along with the brown envelopes stuffed with cash and the reports of all the tribunals, but perhaps that view is a trifle naïve.

Chapter 5

FORGOTTEN BYWAYS IN SOUTH LEINSTER

In the course of delving into the history of Ireland's railways over the course of many years one thing which has become very clear to me is that every line, no matter how apparently unprepossessing or manifestly unsuccessful it was, still has a story to tell. The railways discussed in this chapter bear that out. They were never busy or profitable and they failed to fulfil the aspirations of their promoters, but their story is full of interest and merits recounting. Although this chapter deals with lines built and operated by different companies, their histories became intertwined. The first is that which ran from Bagenalstown (known today as Muine Bheag) to Palace East. The second is the line from Macmine Junction, which was located about 5½ miles south of Enniscorthy on the Dublin to Wexford route, to New Ross which made a junction with the Bagenalstown line at Palace East.

The railway came early to County Carlow. The Act authorising the Great Southern & Western Railway to build its line from Dublin to Cork also included provision for a branch to Carlow, leaving the main line at Cherryville Junction, just west of Kildare. The Carlow branch opened before the main line on 4 August 1846. This line was soon extended beyond Carlow by a new company, the Irish South Eastern Railway, which was closely associated with the GS&WR. The ISER came into existence when two earlier schemes, which had Acts of Parliament but little else to show for their efforts, amalgamated. The first of these, the Great Leinster &

Munster Railway, had been incorporated as long ago as 1837 but had not managed to lay a single yard of track in the intervening years.

The GL&M main line was to run from Dublin to Kilkenny with future extensions to Galway, Cork and Waterford, but the scheme was overtaken by the launch of the GS&WR in 1842. The other line was the Wexford, Carlow & Dublin Junction Railway which proposed a line from the GS&WR's Carlow branch, following the valley of the River Slaney through Bunclody to Wexford. The ISER opened its line as far as Bagenalstown in July 1848 and services were extended to Kilkenny in 1850. This was the second railway to serve Kilkenny. The Waterford & Kilkenny had opened the first part of its route south as far as Thomastown in 1848, and when it reached Dunkitt on the outskirts of Waterford in 1853 through-railway communication between Dublin and Waterford was established.

This put the railway in competition with the existing inland waterway for Dublin to Waterford traffic. Since the middle of the eighteenth century the importance of the River Barrow as a commercial artery had been recognised. Work began in 1749 on improving the river to enable it to be used by barges and other craft. This inched forward painfully slowly over a period of about 30 years and it was not until the 1790s that real progress was made. A long branch off the Grand Canal to Athy opened in 1791 and this led to the formation of the Barrow Navigation Company to create a navigable waterway from there to the tidal reach of the river at St Mullins, a distance of 42 miles. By 1812 the work on the Barrow Navigation was completed and along with the Athy branch of the Grand Canal it provided a waterway connecting Dublin to Waterford. A river valley such as that of the Barrow often offers an easy route for a railway and any line down the valley would be in a position to filch some of the traffic already carried on the navigation. Another attraction of such a line was the prospect of it providing a through route to Wexford as already anticipated by the now defunct WC&DJR, though that line would have run down the valley of the Slaney rather than that of the Barrow.

By 1850 it looked as if the progress on the other obvious route from Dublin to Wexford, that down the east coast, had stalled. Ireland's first railway, the Dublin & Kingstown, which opened in 1834 was extended as far as Dalkey in 1844, using the then revolutionary but ultimately unsuccessful atmospheric system. Carriages were pulled along without locomotives by a piston in a pipe between the rails in which a vacuum was maintained. A lubricated leather seal which closed after the passage of the carriages was supposed to maintain the vacuum created when the air in the pipe was sucked out by a steam engine at a pumping station near the Dalkey terminus. Though the atmospheric railway turned out to be a blind alley in terms of the development of railways, it remained in use for ten years. The fate of this unconventional method of hauling trains was sealed as thoughts turned to extending the line further down the coast towards Bray and beyond.

This was driven by the English Great Western Railway which was anxious to get a share of the trade on the Irish Sea by developing a new port south of Wexford on the Irish side and extending the GWR satellite, the South Wales Railway, to another new port in west Wales. Several companies including the D&K were involved in plans to extend the existing coast line to Bray and open a new inland route from there to a city centre terminus at Harcourt Road. From their junction at Bray, the GWR-backed Waterford, Wexford, Wicklow & Dublin Railway would connect those towns and the new port in County Wexford at Greenore, whose name was later changed to Rosslare. By the time construction got under way, both the Irish companies and the SWR were short of money and the SWR decided not to extend its line beyond Swansea. The great £2 million pound scheme to build lines to Waterford and Wexford was now dropped and in 1851 the Irish company was reconstituted as the Dublin & Wicklow Railway.

When the line to Wicklow was finally opened in 1855 all thoughts of expansion further south to Waterford and Wexford were put on hold. A legacy of this episode, still with us today, was the decision to take the track south from Bray along a coastal route rather than inland. This line was laid out by Isambard Kingdom Brunel, the GWR's engineer. Unquestionably one of the great if flawed geniuses of the Victorian era, nothing seemed impossible to him and in the light of some of his subsequent achievements including designing the biggest steamships of the era, building the railway around Bray Head high above the sea, driving it through tunnels and across wooden trestle bridges, was all in a day's work. Even today from the air-conditioned comfort of a DART electric train one cannot but marvel at the work that went into building and maintaining this line. Observant passengers will also see from the windows of their train the work which railway engineers following in Brunel's footsteps have had to carry out to move the alignment inland from the sea as the forces of nature have wreaked havoc on the great engineer's original route.

With the WWW&D in difficulties, promoters' thoughts turned again to a revival of an inland route to Wexford such as that planned by the WC&DJ. This led to the establishment of the Bagenalstown & Wexford Railway which was authorised in 1854 to build a railway from a junction with the GS&WR's Carlow line at Bagenalstown down the valley of the River Barrow and then across to Enniscorthy and Wexford. This scheme had the backing of the GS&WR and the ISER. The ISER chairman, John Redmond, a banker and ship owner who was to sit as the MP for Wexford from 1859 to 1865, was appointed chairman of the B&W. He was a member of that great political dynasty which served Wexford for many decades and whose eponymous ancestor was to deliver Home Rule to Ireland after many years of struggle in 1914 only for subsequent events to turn this great achievement to dust. Tangible support for the scheme came from the GS&WR in the form of a subscription of £50,000.

The company was strongly supported by local landowners and one of these, Arthur MacMurrough Kavanagh, deserves more than a footnote in history. His family claimed ancestry back to Diarmuid MacMurrough, the twelfth-century High King of Leinster who invited Henry II and Strongbow to take an interest in Irish affairs and who thus can be blamed to some degree for kicking off the ructions which marked the next 800 years. Arthur was born in 1831, fourth in line to the family's extensive estates, but he was severely handicapped with little more than stumps for hands and legs. Despite his disabilities, he learned to ride a horse and engaged in the pursuits beloved of most country gentlemen of his class. He could shoot, follow the hounds and fish. Between 1846 and 1853, he travelled extensively in Egypt, Persia and India in the company of his older brother Thomas, suffering all kinds of dangers and privations. Thomas died of consumption in 1852 and in the following year his other surviving brother Charles was killed in a fire, leaving Arthur as heir to the family estates and the splendid family seat, Borris House. He returned to Ireland and in 1855 married a cousin, Mary, with whom he had six children. Kavanagh was a conservative but enlightened landlord who later served as an MP for both the counties of Carlow and Wexford and saw the coming of the railway as a great benefit for the districts it served. The line passed through his estates for 14 miles and Kavanagh is reputed by his biographer to have given the land required for the railway to the company free of charge.

The cutting of the first sod to signal the start of the construction of the Bagenalstown & Wexford Railway took place at Borris in January 1855, the ceremonial spade being wielded by Kavanagh's mother, Lady Harriet. The contract to build the first section of the line from Bagenalstown to Borris was awarded to J.J. Bagnell. The formation of the line as built gives substance to the view that it was intended to be more than a country branch line. It was built to take double track, though only one was ever laid. The route chosen was to the east of the River Barrow in the shadow of the Blackstairs Mountains and involved some severe

1. One of the engines that was used on the narrow gauge line from Ballymena to Parkmore is being coaled at Ballymena. Wicker baskets such as that seen on the coaling stage on the right of the picture were often used for this task. The locomotive, No 102, a 2-4-2 tank engine, was built at York Road works in Belfast in 1908, and survived until 1954 when it was scrapped following the closure of the branch from Ballymoney to Ballycastle, the final 3ft gauge line in County Antrim. (*Author's collection*)

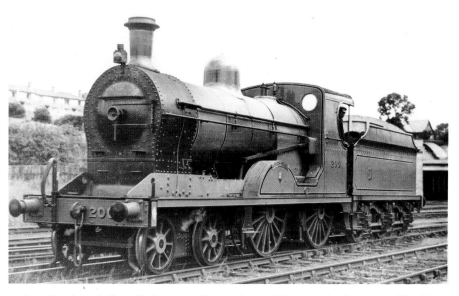

2. Great Northern Railway U class 4-4-0 No 200 *Lough Melvin*, resplendent in sky-blue livery, awaits her next turn of duty at Clones. Part of the distinctive roundhouse type of engine shed, common elsewhere in Europe, but one of only two in Ireland (the other was at Portadown Junction also on the GNR) can be seen behind the engine. (*Author's collection*)

3. One of the delights of the GNR lines which closed in 1957 was the famous Fintona horse tram. Here a gelding called Dick, the final specimen from a long line of equine motive power which had been hauling the tram since the 1850s, is ready to leave the station in the village to head to Fintona Junction some three quarters of a mile distant. (*Author's collection*)

4. A goods from Portadown bound for Derry passes through Donaghmore station in County Tyrone on the erstwhile GNR's Derry Road. The line carried quite heavy goods traffic right up to the end, though by the time this picture was taken, in June 1964, the station had been closed. The locomotive is former GNR SG2 class 0-6-0 No 16 renumbered 38 by the UTA. (*Des Fitzgerald*)

5. A relic of the fabled *Bundoran Express* survived until the last summer of the Derry Road in the form of a CIÉ train which brought pilgrims bound for Lough Derg as far as Omagh station from whence they continued their journey by bus. The return working is seen on the climb out of Omagh hauled by CIÉ General Motors diesel locomotive B171. Not long arrived from the USA when this view was taken, most of these long-lived and successful locomotives remained in service with Iarnród Éireann well into the new millennium. (*Geoff Lumb*)

6. A couple of U class 4-4-0 locomotives simmer outside the GNR engine shed at Enniskillen in June 1957, a few months before all of the lines through the county town of Fermanagh were swept off the railway map of Ireland. The line to the left of the signal box led to Clones while the SL&NCR route to Sligo curves off to the right. (*Author's collection*)

7. One of the SL&NCR tricomposite bogie coaches, which contained seating for all three classes of passenger, is seen in the sidings at Enniskillen awaiting its next trip to Sligo. This line was a law unto itself in so many ways. On every railway carriage in which I have ever travelled the door handles were on the right; on this line they were on the left. (*Author's collection*)

8. GNR U class 4-4-0 No 199 *Lough Derg*, an appropriately named locomotive for this duty, slowly edges the up or Dublin bound *Bundoran Express* round the sharp curve through Enniskillen station in August 1957. (*Author's collection*)

9. A few weeks before the demise of the SL&NCR in September 1957 *Sir Henry* brings a long goods from Enniskillen into Manorhamilton. The number of wagons behind the 1904-built locomotive perhaps suggests that the locals were stocking up before the line closed and all the railway's goods and livestock traffic was thrown arbitrarily onto the totally inadequate roads of the border counties which it had served since 1882. (*Author's collection*)

10. Gleaming SL&NCR 0-6-4 tank engine *Lissadell* poses for the photographer on the turntable at Sligo in the 1930s. This locomotive was built in Manchester by Beyer Peacock in 1899 and was withdrawn from service in 1954. (*Author's collection*)

11. A view of Dundalk Square Crossing where the line from Greenore crossed over the double track Dublin to Belfast main line. The crossing was situated south of Dundalk station just in front of the GNR works which were located behind the photographer. (*Author's collection*)

12. LNWR saddletank No 2 *Greenore* leaves the station she was named after with a passenger train. No 2 was built at Crewe works in 1873 for the opening of the line and was not scrapped until 1951. (*Author's collection*)

13. Seen at Dundalk, No 5 *Carlingford*, in the condition in which she was delivered in 1876, heads a complete LNWR train on Irish soil. The locomotive's cab does not have a roof, though one was later provided. Her many sisters across the Irish Sea were used mostly as shunting locomotives. On such duties the lack of a roof, while hardly agreeable for the crew, might just have been about tolerable. The unfortunate drivers and firemen who had to drive them from Greenore to Dundalk and Newry must have got quite a battering when gales swept in from the sea. (*Author's collection*)

14. No 6 *Holyhead*, the locomotive involved in the 1904 accident at Greenore, was captured here on the other part of the system, at Newry's Edward Street station. (*Author's collection*)

15. A view of Macmine Junction where the lines from Bagenalstown and New Ross met the Dublin to Wexford and Rosslare route. The branch trains normally used the left-hand side of the island platform. (*John Langford*)

16. On 17 December 1959, a passenger train from Waterford to Wexford via New Ross hauled by J9 class 0-6-0 No 354 approaches Palace East. The line to Bagenalstown, which still saw seasonal use for sugar beet traffic, is to the right of the train. (*John Langford*)

17. The now preserved J15 class 0-6-0 No 186 is seen at New Ross in December 1959 hauling the 10.00am passenger train from Wexford to Waterford. (*John Langford*)

18. Sugar beet traffic kept many lines in the Irish Republic open long after they had lost their passenger services. With the impressive ruins of its Franciscan abbey as a backdrop, wagons are loaded with sugar beet at Timoleague in the autumn of 1960. The whole of the former CB&SCR system was closed the following year. (*John Phillips*)

19. Even though CIÉ provided modern motive power for the west Cork lines in the 1950s, this did not prevent their demise. This brand new CIÉ C class diesel C217 was recorded at Skibbereen in August 1957 with a passenger train. (*Richard D Kehm*)

20. The sun sets over Baltimore in July 1957 as a new silver liveried diesel, again C217, is in marked contrast to the elderly six-wheeled coach which is the first vehicle of her train. (*Richard D Kehm*)

21. A sight all too common in Ireland in the last fifty years was the lifting train. Here one of the famous Bandon tanks, No 463, is an accomplice to the destruction of the railway that she had been built to serve. This scene was recorded near Bantry in June 1962. (*John Phillips*)

22. Carrying the initials of a railway company which never really existed, the L&BER, 4-6-oT No 3 was one of the quartet of small engines which the Board of Works deemed adequate to work the lengthy Burtonport line. Built by Andrew Barclay in Scotland in 1902, No 3 survived until 1954. (*Author's collection*)

23. Proper locomotives for the L&BER finally arrived in 1905 with the pair of 4-8-0 tender locomotives, Nos 11 and 12. The latter is seen here outside the shed at Letterkenny which was built with money provided by the Scotter award which settled—at least for a few years—the war between the Board of Works and the L&LSR. The line to the right of the engine shed provided a connection between the Swilly and the County Donegal Railway's branch to Letterkenny from Strabane. (*Author's collection*)

24. GSR No 532, seen in the sidings at Westport, was one of the legendary Achill bogies which were used on the branch throughout its existence. Built in 1900 by the MGWR at the Broadstone in Dublin, it was originally named *Britannia*. The GSR renumbered all the locomotives it inherited from its constituent companies and removed their nameplates. No 532 lasted much longer than the Achill branch, being withdrawn by CIÉ in 1949. (*Courtesy Charles Friel*)

25. The brooding remains of the Owencarrow viaduct still stalk across the valley to this day. The stone arches, the scene of the fatal accident in 1925 when carriages were blown off the track, can be seen in the foreground. (*Author*)

26. On 24 September 1953, J15 0-6-0 No 156 is seen at the station at Valentia Harbour. The GSR bi-lingual nameboard referred to in the text is in the foreground. The J15s—118 of them were built between 1866 and 1903—were by far Ireland's most numerous class of steam locomotives and were associated with the line throughout its existence. No 156 was an early member of the class built at Inchicore in 1871. It was not withdrawn until 1961. (*Courtesy Charles Friel*)

27. On 13 May 1953, the 2.10pm service from Valentia to Farranfore headed by a J15 begins its slow progress across Gleensk viaduct. The check rails which were laid across the viaduct to minimise the risk of derailment can be seen in the photograph. (*Courtesy Charles Friel*)

gradients. There were two significant and expensive engineering features on the line, a deep rock cutting at Kilcoltrim and the magnificent 16-arch viaduct at Borris. This was designed by the line's engineer, another interesting character. He was William Le Fanu, a graduate of Trinity College whose more famous brother, Sheridan Le Fanu, was a much-read Victorian novelist famed for ghost stories and what have since been described as gothic novels. William Le Fanu himself showed some literary talent and his book, *Seventy Years of Irish Life*, published in 1893 the year before he died is a hugely enjoyable pot-pourri of stories and anecdotes ranging from tales of fishing trips to faction fights and meetings with famous contemporaries such as Anthony Trollope and William Dargan.

One of Le Fanu's first railway jobs was as an assistant engineer when the Dublin to Cork line was being built and he tells a particularly alarming tale which is probably all too typical of some of the practices of that early phase of railway construction. One evening Le Fanu had arranged to get a lift on one of the contractor's engines from Limerick Junction to Charleville where he was staying. Alarmed at the great speed at which the young driver, who worked for William Dargan the contractor, was making on the temporary track, Le Fanu cautioned him to slow down. At this point the driver told him that another engine was scheduled along the same track that evening in the other direction and that they had to get to Charleville before it departed in case they met it head on. The thought of waiting for the other engine to get to Limerick Junction before they left or turning back did not seem to have occurred to him. They did reach Charleville in one piece just as the other engine was about to leave!

The line opened as far as Borris in December 1858 with the services, which consisted of only two trains each way daily, being worked by the GS&WR on behalf of the B&W. Almost from the beginning the line was operated at a loss. By now the powers in the original Act had lapsed so another visit to parliament was required in 1859 to get an extension to the time allowed to build the rest of the line. The contract for the next section, from Borris to Ballywilliam, was awarded to one Peter O'Reilly—the only occasion this name appears as a railway contractor probably because he was declared bankrupt in April 1861. J.J. Bagnell had to be brought back to complete the work, which included the great viaduct at Borris. Made from granite quarried in the vicinity, its 16 spans were 35 ft across, and took the track some 70 ft over the river below.

It was not until March 1862 that the 6½ miles to Ballywilliam were opened but no further progress was attempted with the financial resources of the company by now exhausted. The line was worked by the GS&WR but as it went really from nowhere to nowhere receipts were poor and the losses continued. In 1862 revenue was only £1,772 while the cost of working the line was £2,582. The B&W was soon being assailed by its creditors. These included William Le Fanu who in 1863 successfully sued the company for £5,000. The GS&WR continued to work the line until the end of 1863 when it withdrew. As the B&W had no rolling stock of its own, services ended. With no revenue, or prospects of any, the company was declared bankrupt in June 1864 with debts of over £100,000. In 1865 it seemed as if the B&W had finally and irretrievably hit the buffers when parliament passed an Act, 'authorizing the Sale by the Assignees in Bankruptcy of the Estate and Effects of the Bagenalstown and Wexford Railway Company of their Line of Railway and all other of their Property, together with the Rights, Powers, Authorities, and Privileges of the said Company, and for the Dissolution of the said Company.'

Just when it seemed that the line was finished, an unlikely saviour came riding over the horizon. This was one Standish H. Motte, a barrister based in London. His initial involvement seems to have been as the lawyer representing some of the creditors of the B&W. Though he had family connections with the area and owned land in the counties of both Wexford and Carlow, Motte had no apparent previous connection with the world of railways, though as a parliamentary draftsman he would have assisted in the preparation of many of the railway bills which came before parliament. He was a member of an organisation called the Aboriginal Protection Society which was active in the 1840s and wrote a pamphlet which was remarkably foresighted and liberal for the time, protesting against the exploitation of indigenous peoples in the British Empire and proposing what was almost a charter to protect them and give them some recourse to legal redress if wronged by colonists.

There can be no denying that this London lawyer was an unlikely railway proprietor and if he had been acting for the creditors of the B&W one might have thought he would have had more sense than to try and resuscitate its corpse, but that is precisely what he did. When the B&W was put up for auction by order of the Bankruptcy Court in January 1866, Motte bought it for only £25,000. It had cost the company over £20,000 to build the Borris viaduct alone. Then in August 1866, Motte obtained an act which incorporated the Waterford, New Ross & Wexford Junction Railway Company.

By now over 12 years had elapsed since the B&W had been launched and in the intervening years the coastal route had gradually been extended towards Wexford. The Dublin & Wicklow had restyled itself as the Dublin, Wicklow & Wexford in an Act of 1859 and its line reached Enniscorthy by 1863, though it would be a further nine years before its trains finally got as far as Wexford. The WNR&W planned to build two lines 34 miles in extent. One was to run from Ballywilliam, which was as far as the B&W had got, through New Ross to Waterford. The other would head east to meet the DW&W's extension to Wexford at a place which became known as Macmine Junction. Quite what Motte hoped to achieve by building these lines is hard to fathom. The existing route from Waterford to Dublin was well established and the new DW&W line would be a shorter and much quicker means of getting from Wexford to Dublin than the line through Borris. All that could reasonably be expected from these proposed new lines was local traffic and that had hardly proved profitable to date.

Construction first began on the line eastwards towards Macmine Junction with the help of a loan of £60,000 from the Public Works Loan Commissioners. The contractors, Edgeworth & Stamford, were also given the task of putting the Bagenalstown to Ballywilliam line back into working order. As the company possessed only one locomotive, an ancient relic built for the Midland Great Western in 1847 which it had acquired from its contractors, the GS&WR was asked to work the line. Train services were resumed from Bagenalstown through Borris to a terminus at Mackmine, about a mile from the eventual junction with the DW&W, in the autumn of 1870. The switchback nature of the Ballywilliam to Mackmine line suggests that it was built on the cheap but without the connection to the Wexford line which had not yet been completed or the line to New Ross and Waterford which had not even been started, once again, as with the B&W before it, the WNR&W was going from nowhere to nowhere. The final part of the WNR&W from its temporary terminus to Macmine Junction opened in May 1873 but in September of the same year, on the advice of its engineer who declared the line unsafe, the GS&WR withdrew the services it was providing and this ill-fated line closed yet again.

By now Motte's passion for railway building and perhaps his money had been spent and in 1874 he seems to have withdrawn from his less than successful career as a railway magnate in Ireland and returned to his work as a barrister in London. Motte was replaced as chairman of the WNR&W by Arthur MacMurrough Kavanagh who at this time was the MP for Carlow. In January 1874 Kavanagh asked the GS&WR to resume working the line and, though they declined, the company agreed to hire an engine and rolling stock to the WNR&W so that they could do it themselves. Services began again in February 1874 with Kavanagh himself paying the fees to the GS&WR for the hired rolling stock in order to keep the line open. In 1875 he tried unsuccessfully to persuade the DW&W to buy the line but in the face of mounting losses its biggest creditor, the Public Works Loan Commissioners, announced that it would be put up for auction. In 1876 the line was sold to the GS&WR and the DW&WR for a total of £40,000. The boundary between the two new owning companies was at Ballywilliam, with the line north being the property of the GS&WR. For some years the DW&W exercised powers to run trains from Macmine Junction as far as Bagenalstown, but the route never saw the through services to Dublin which had once been the aspiration of the original promoters.

This was not the end of the story as the plans of the WNR&W line for a line to New Ross and Waterford were realised by the DW&W. The GS&WR were consulted about a possible extension to New Ross and Waterford in 1876 but declined to become involved, so in 1877 the DW&W sought and obtained an Act for a line from Palace East to New Ross. The following year the Waterford Extension Act was passed authorising the extension of this line from New Ross to Waterford. This ambitious and expensive scheme which involved a bridge across the River Suir to connect with the line to Mallow was never pursued, and no works were undertaken on the Palace East to New Ross section either for another seven years. It was not until 1884 that a contract to build the branch to New Ross was awarded to Robert Worthington.

This line, which was less than 8 miles in extent, was nonetheless a difficult one from an engineering point of view. Leaving New Ross the branch crossed the River Barrow on a 590 ft long five-span steel girder bridge. One of these could be opened to allow river traffic to pass underneath and there was a cabin on the County Waterford side of the river to control the opening span. Immediately after crossing the river, the line plunged into the 745 yard long Mount Elliot tunnel. It then climbed continuously for over 5 miles through deep rock cuttings and on high embankments, with locomotives having to cope with gradients as steep as 1 in 60 before they reached Palace East which at 480 ft above sea level was the highest point on the DW&W system. The only intermediate station, at Rathgarogue, was added six years after the line opened in 1887. The line was eventually extended the

14 miles from New Ross to Waterford in 1904.

Therefore, from 1887, Palace East became a junction. The agreement between the DW&W and the GS&WR when they had jointly bought the former B&W and WNR&W lines had given ownership of the route as far as Ballywilliam to the DW&W. With the opening of the New Ross line this left the DW&W responsible for this short stub of track only 3½ miles long. In 1902, the DW&W transferred this to the GS&WR. From that time on the DW&W provided a service from Macmine Junction to New Ross, and the connecting GS&WR trains to Bagenalstown started from a bay platform at Palace East. An extant timetable from 1881 when the DW&W was working the Bagenalstown line shows only two through trains which left Macmine Junction at 9.00am and 12.45pm, taking two hours to cover the 35 miles. There was an additional evening service at 6.00pm; this only ran as far as Ballywilliam and was advertised in the timetable as Ballywilliam for New Ross. A horse-drawn carriage ran to New Ross, connecting with the trains at Ballywilliam.

In 1900 there was a generous service of four GS&WR trains on the Bagenalstown to Ballywilliam line. One of these ran only as far as Borris almost in the style of a commuter service, arriving at 7.35am from Bagenalstown and returning at 7.40am, though scholars rather than workers may have been the main users of this train. The other three ran through to Ballywilliam. Once the GS&WR took over the working of the line through to Palace East services settled down to the familiar pattern of two or three trains per day which sufficed for most minor Irish lines. The summer timetable for 1922 shows a rather different pattern of services, with three trains running each way between Bagenalstown and Borris but only one going through to Palace East. There was a good reason for this, to which we will return presently.

For the opening of the Macmine Junction to New Ross line in 1887 three through passenger trains were provided, though by 1900 this had increased to five or six trains per day in each direction. There were four trains scheduled daily in 1922 between

Waterford and Macmine Junction via New Ross, the extension of the line to Waterford having fully opened in April 1904, though how often the full service actually ran in those troubled times is open to question. The lines of the Dublin & South Eastern Railway, as the DW&W had been renamed in 1906, were subject to many attacks and severe disruption during the Civil War. County Wexford was a rebel stronghold and there was a catalogue of train wrecking, ambushes and arson attacks, much of which was focused on the D&SER main line between Enniscorthy and Wexford and on the New Ross branch. The company had to resort in 1922 to issuing amended timetables every few months to take account of the latest incidents of damage to its lines with the resulting disruption to its services. Some of the worst of these occurred between Palace East and New Ross in 1923. Given the troubled conditions in this part of County Wexford one can understand the GS&WR's reluctance to allow more than one service to venture as far as Palace East at this time.

On 10 January the scheduled 4.15pm mixed passenger and goods train from Enniscorthy to Waterford was heavily laden with 26 wagons of pigs in addition to the normal two passenger coaches and needed two engines to haul it. When it reached the isolated station of Rathgarogue, the only one between Palace East and New Ross, it was hijacked by insurgents. One engine was detached and the driver was forced to take it about a mile west of the station. The wagons of livestock were detached from the remaining engine and the passenger coaches before these were sent off to collide with the engine out on the line. When the empty passenger train hit the stationary engine both locomotives were badly damaged and somehow the first locomotive became detached from its tender which was destroyed in the smash. With the force of the impact the tender-less and of course driverless locomotive set off on its own and because the line from Rathgarogue to New Ross was steeply downhill all the way, it careered into Mount Elliot tunnel, across the Barrow Bridge and through New Ross station only coming to a halt near Glenmore station, having travelled close to 10 miles on its own, crashing through several sets of level crossing gates which were hindering its progress on the way.

Another incident occurred 10 days later on the morning of 20 January 1923 when anti-treaty forces took control of Palace East station and two trains which happened to be there at the time, a goods from Waterford and the morning passenger train from Macmine Junction to Waterford. There must have been rogue railwaymen among their numbers for they seemed to know how to drive or at least start a steam locomotive. The engine of the passenger train was first sent off back towards Macmine Junction. The rebels then detached some wagons containing more livestock from the goods before setting the rest of the train off without a driver to crash into the other engine, which it duly did—blocking the line with two damaged engines and a pile of wreckage from the wagons. The two engines involved were only fit for scrap after the crash. Whilst they were more than happy to cause as much destruction as possible to the railways, I suppose the insurgents' concern for the welfare of the pigs caught up in both episodes merits some recognition. They were probably mostly farmers' sons who would have appreciated the value of the pigs if not of the railways.

With the effective ending of the Civil War in May 1923, some stability at last returned to the country. In 1925 the railways in the Free State were amalgamated to form the GSR and the first priority of the new company was to repair all the damage that had occurred during the years of conflict. However, the railways were now operating in a changed landscape in economic as well as political terms and they were being subjected to serious and initially unregulated competition for the first time in the shape of cars, buses and lorries. In order to counter this, rates for goods and livestock were cut but this did little to improve the GSR's finances. It was a private company with shareholders. Before the war, railway shares would have been a part of many investment portfolios, and whereas shares in the bigger companies at least would have produced dividends then, there were no dividends now for holders of GSR stock. The worldwide trade slump after the Wall Street crash and later the economic war with Britain exacerbated an already difficult situation.

The company was barely solvent at the start of the 1930s and it is sometimes forgotten that the first significant contraction of Ireland's railway network took place in that decade. Passenger services between Palace East and Bagenalstown were an early casualty of this first phase of retrenchment, being withdrawn at the end of January 1931. Despite this setback, the line remained theoretically open for some traffic for another 32 years. Goods trains continued to run until April 1944 when they succumbed to wartime coal shortages, not resuming until December 1945. Regular scheduled goods services were suspended again owing to coal shortages in January 1947 and were never restarted. However, occasional livestock specials and sugar beet traffic kept the line just about alive until complete closure by CIÉ in April 1963.

As the cultivation of that humble root vegetable, *beta vulgaris*, known to those of us devoid of a classical education or training in botany as sugar beet, played a major role in the survival of many Irish railway lines including the one through Borris, which would otherwise have disappeared much earlier, a word or two on its significance may be relevant here. The discovery that sugar could be produced from beet grown in Europe as well as from cane produced in warmer climes dates back to the eighteenth century. There was an abortive attempt to introduce the crop and the industry to Ireland in the mid-nineteenth century with a factory at Mountmellick in the 1850s. Then in 1926 a Belgian company opened a plant in Carlow to process sugar beet. This too failed but the Irish government stepped in to establish Comhlucht Siuicre Éireann (the Irish Sugar Company) and other factories were built at Mallow, Tuam and Thurles and, equally importantly, farmers were encouraged to grow sugar beet. By the early 1940s, the Free State was self sufficient in sugar and every autumn the railways were involved in running hundreds of specials to take the crop to the sugar factories. Slumbering branches such as the Bagenalstown to Palace East line sprang into life for a few months as elderly locomotives slowly hauled long trains of equally elderly wagons loaded with sugar beet towards the various factories.

The factories at Tuam and Thurles were closed in the early 1980s but those at Carlow and Mallow continued to flourish. At the peak of sugar beet production, close to 100,000 acres were under cultivation with the crop. The industry was privatised in 1991 but the two remaining factories carried on until the closure of the Carlow plant in 2005. Then, in 2006, Greencore, the present owners of the former Comhlucht Siuicre Éireann suddenly announced that the Mallow factory would close in May of that year in the face of the withdrawal of EU subsidies and with it went the whole industry. The last beet campaign as it was known on the railways was that of the autumn of 2005. For many years the only traffic flow was from a mechanised loading plant at Wellington Bridge on the South Wexford line to Mallow via Clonmel and Limerick Junction. CIÉ/IR had commendably provided more modern, fully-braked wagons for this seasonal traffic and in the end it was the closure of the industry which lost the railway one of its few remaining freight flows, rather than the other way around which was more usual.

Passenger services lasted much longer on the line from Macmine Junction to New Ross and Waterford. Though wartime coal shortages saw passenger trains withdrawn from the line in April 1944, they resumed the next year, only to be suspended again due to severe coal shortages during that bitter winter of 1947. The service was restored again when the coal stocks improved in June of that year. The summer timetable dating from June 1950 offered two through trains each way from Macmine Junction to Waterford and one additional service each way between Waterford and New Ross. The two trains from Waterford had connections at Macmine Junction to both Dublin and Wexford and there were also connections there from Rosslare and Wexford with the services heading west to Waterford. Even though most

CIÉ passenger services were in the hands of diesel traction by the end of the 1950s, a few pockets of steam remained into the 1960s. One of these was around Wexford and Waterford. Steam locomotives were used both in the course of the sugar beet campaign in the autumn and often on passenger services on the New Ross line. The line from Macmine Junction to New Ross closed completely from 1 April 1963, the same day the line north from Palace East finally succumbed. Regular goods traffic on the section from Waterford to New Ross ended in September 1976 during the next wave of closures, though some fertiliser traffic continued to use the line into the 1980s.

There were few lines in the history of Ireland's railways which were less successful than that which ran south from Bagenalstown into County Wexford. Though it was originally promoted as a through route from Dublin to Wexford it never came close to achieving that early objective. Even if the company had been able to raise the funds to enable it to build a line through to Wexford in the 1850s, the eventual extension of the much shorter and quicker line down the east coast would have reduced it to the status of a secondary route. With the benefit of hindsight, which is always a great help when it comes to reviewing some of the follies of our ancestors, it is hard to see where its promoters thought its traffic would come from, serving as it did a sparsely populated rural area. In the end its most remarkable claim to fame was that it survived into the 1960s, though by that time it was only used for the seasonal beet traffic. Even though it was closed down several times in the nineteenth century, on every occasion it somehow struggled back to life.

The whole line probably cost close to £500,000 to build and yet it is doubtful if it ever made a profit in any of the over 100 years it remained in use. There are many hundreds of miles of railways throughout Ireland which should never have been closed. However, in the case of the route of the Bagenalstown & Wexford Railway, we have a rare example of a line that should probably never have been built in the first place. The existence of the B&W

to some extent begat the line to New Ross which at least served a town and a port of some significance and eventually was to reach the city of Waterford, though this never provided a realistic alternative to the long-established route from there to Dublin via Kilkenny.

Today, there are probably still rails buried under the best part of 30 years of untamed growth between New Ross and Abbey Junction in Waterford but you would be hard pushed to find them. The track was lifted after closure between New Ross and Macmine Junction and between Palace East and Bagenalstown. The bridge over the Barrow was dismantled and only the very observant will be able to detect what little remains of the site of Macmine Junction from a railcar speeding to or from Wexford and Rosslare. Nature and the hand of man have combined to obliterate most traces of the two lines in the more than four decades since they closed. The station building and platform at Goresbridge are extant as is the cottage provided for the custodian of the adjacent level crossing, Goresbridge Station Gates, though both are virtually derelict. Goresbridge station is quite an unprepossessing affair in contrast to two of the other surviving stations.

The next one down the line from Goresbridge, that at Borris, which is in private hands and the cottage provided for the family in charge of nearby Borris Crossing are in quite a different league, in terms of their architecture. Both are made from smooth cut stone and have high ornate chimneys which probably owe their inspiration to Tudor style country houses. Perhaps it was felt that something a bit special had to be provided at the station which was used by Arthur MacMurrough Kavanagh and those visiting the nearby Borris House. One other extant station on the line is even more impressive. The station building at Ballywilliam is a huge two-storey affair with four massive chimneys. It is much larger than many of the stations provided for sizeable towns throughout Ireland. How the directors of an impecunious concern like the B&W ever imagined that a building as big as this was required at such a place is hard to fathom.

However, the most impressive surviving relic of the illfated B&W is Borris viaduct. The village is still dominated by this magnificent structure which stands as proud and majestic today as when the final stone was set in the last of its 16 arches. It is a fitting memorial to the shades of the remarkable Arthur MacMurrough Kavanagh, Motte the deluded barrister and its creator William Le Fanu. Maybe I am just a hopeless railway romantic but I fancy that the viaduct at Borris will still be admired long after people have forgotten all about his once more illustrious brother's novels.

Chapter 6 ⌥

CLOSED AT THE STROKE OF A PEN: THE DESTRUCTION OF WEST CORK'S RAILWAYS

M any years ago several different people told me variations on a story that concerned the closure in 1961 of the railway lines in the west of County Cork which were formally operated by the Cork, Bandon & South Coast Railway. I had always assumed, perhaps hoped is a better word, that the story was apocryphal but having since seen it in print, albeit with a caveat as to its veracity—it is recounted in Mícheál Ó Riain's masterful history of CIÉ, *On The Move*, published by Gill & Macmillan in 1995—I feel able to repeat it here. The story goes that in 1960, after much prevarication over an agenda for a meeting, Todd Andrews, the head of CIÉ, finally agreed to meet a deputation from west Cork protesting about his proposed closure of all the railway lines which served their area. Andrews' position was that he was happy to have a meeting to discuss the alternative bus and lorry services that would be introduced following the closure of the railways but was not prepared to discuss the closure proposal itself. In the face of growing political pressure, he eventually agreed to meet the deputation at the CIÉ offices at Kingsbridge station. After the initial pleasantries had been conducted Andrews asked the delegates protesting against the closure of their rail services for their rail tickets so that he could make some arrangements concerning their return journey. He found, what he probably had guessed or had known beforehand, that none of them had such a thing as a railway ticket—they had all come to Dublin by car.

In fairness to the delegation, such was the level of service provided on the West Cork lines it would have been impossible to make a round trip to Dublin from Bandon, Bantry, Skibbereen or Baltimore and back in the one day. Even though the operation of both passenger and goods services on these lines had been modernised by CIÉ and were largely in the hands of diesel locomotives and railcars since their introduction in the mid-1950s, in the narrowly focused logic of the time this railway was losing money and had to be closed. The fate of the former CB&SCR system was even more comprehensive than that of the GNR lines in the north where at least something remained after the events of 1957. In the case of the West Cork lines, for the first time in Ireland the complete route mileage of a once significant railway company was swept off the map, at the stroke of a pen.

The wielder of that pen, Dr C.S. (commonly known as Todd allegedly because of his resemblance to a cartoon character of that name) Andrews, who was made Chairman of CIÉ in 1958, was a far cry from the traditional railway manager. In the context of the Ireland of the time he was seen as a technocrat and a moderniser. He was the man who had established Bord na Móna as a significant force in the Irish economy, developing facilities across the country to harvest and process peat for use both to generate electricity and as a horticultural product. Given Andrews' subsequent career at CIÉ, there is a certain irony that Bord na Móna relied heavily on narrow gauge railways to bring the peat from the bogs to the power stations and processing plants. Their network of both permanent and temporary 3 ft gauge lines is today probably in the region of 1,500 route miles, making it the biggest railway operator on the island of Ireland, by some distance. With his background as an active republican as a young man, Andrews may have got his taste for destroying railways during the Civil War, but he was close to the new elite in the Irish Republic and his appointment to CIÉ was directly at the behest of the Taoiseach, Seán Lemass. Andrews was a contradictory figure in the sense that while he was a modern man and a highly effective manager and entrepreneur, he was still a part of that self-serving and self-promoting network with its roots in Civil War politics, which was as unedifying and excluding as that which operated in Northern Ireland at the time for very different reasons.

Even if he had reservations about the railway closure programme which was driven through during his time as the Chairman of CIÉ and with which he will forever be associated, and I am not aware that he had any, Andrews really had no alternative but to go along with it. The company had been fully state-owned since 1950 and it was the clear policy of the governments of the time to make public transport pay its way. This was the Holy Grail which politicians both north and south of the border had been seeking for many years. As the railways were the biggest contributors to the losses of the respective nationalised public transport operators on both sides of the border, they had to suffer the biggest cuts. It would be a long time before it dawned on any of those politicians or their successors in that sometimes ignoble profession that this prize would be as impossible to find as the elusive Grail. For the rest of us, the damage done to the national railway network in the course of their futile quest is largely irreversible.

The railway network which served West Cork and was closed by Todd Andrews in 1961 had taken over 50 years to build. The impetus for the first railway seems to have come not from Cork city but from the town of Bandon where a meeting was held in September 1844. A provisional committee was formed, surveys of potential traffic were conducted and moves were begun to secure parliamentary approval for the project. Royal assent was received in July 1845 for the Act authorising the construction of the Cork & Bandon Railway, the company being empowered to raise

£200,000 to build the line. The *London Illustrated News* reported on a great junket held in September 1845 in a specially built pavilion in a field beside the Bandon River to celebrate the cutting of the first sod. The Earl of Bandon wielded the ceremonial spade to the accompaniment of cheers from a crowd of several thousand before his lordship and invited guests retired to take lunch.

Once the festivities were over, work began on the construction of the railway. The line from the C&B station in the centre of Cork on Albert Quay to Bandon was about 17 miles long but it proved challenging from an engineering point of view. There were two major engineering features, the 90 ft high Chetwynd viaduct which took the line over the Cork to Bandon road on four 110 ft spans and Ireland's first significant railway tunnel, the 906 yards long Ballinhassig (or Gogginshill as it was sometimes called) tunnel. At first progress on the works was slow and the company's engineer, Edmund Leahy, paid the price for this with his dismissal in 1846. Eventually in June 1849 the first part of the line from Bandon to Ballinhassig was passed fit for service and trains began to run on that section. Passengers were taken forward from Ballinhassig to Cork by horse-drawn omnibuses, pending completion of the line into the city. Difficulties with the tunnel, the Chetwynd viaduct and the construction of a long embankment at Ballyphehane across boggy ground all conspired to delay the opening.

When the line was more or less complete, a row between the company and its contractors, Fox, Henderson & Company, blew up, literally. The contractors claimed they were owed an additional £30,000 by the company. When payment was not forthcoming they resolved to stop the imminent opening of the line. In August 1851 some of the contractors' men used dynamite to blast tons of rock and spoil from the sides of two cuttings on to the track, causing serious blockages. The Board of Trade official who came to Cork shortly after this outbreak of insanity to inspect the line prior to its opening was unable to travel along it and the opening was postponed until December of that year. Initially four trains were provided each way between Cork and Bandon on weekdays, with two on Sundays.

The line from Cork to Bandon was now at least operational but the company was in serious financial trouble. The C&B had cost around £20,000 per mile to construct. A loan of £35,000 at 5 per cent interest had had to be obtained from the Public Works Loan Commissioners in 1850 to enable the line to be completed and such was the state of the company's finances it struggled to meet the repayments on this. The demands of the Public Works Loan Commissioners and other creditors brought the C&B close to bankruptcy several times in the mid-1850s. The line to Bandon had cost a fortune to build but was too short to generate enough traffic to be profitable, so almost at once thoughts were turned to extensions further west. Powers were obtained in an Act of 1853 to allow the company to raise another £280,000 to build a 32 mile long extension to Bantry and a branch to Clonakilty, and a further Act of 1854 authorised a branch from Drimoleague on the new line to Skibbereen. None of these lines was built and the powers given in these Acts lapsed. In fact nothing happened for many years and it was not until the next decade that the first extension to the system was opened.

This was an 11 mile long branch from what became Kinsale Junction (with a startling lack of imagination it was named simply Junction from 1863 until 1888) to the busy fishing port of Kinsale. It was promoted and built by an independent company, the Cork & Kinsale Junction Railway, though it had several C&B directors on its board. The Bandon company agreed to work the new line for 30 per cent of its receipts. The branch opened in June 1863 but receipts were disappointing and the contractors who built it forced the company into receivership in June 1864 for the non-payment of monies owed to them. Following some restructuring of its finances, the C&KR came out of receivership in 1868 but it was back in that condition again in 1872. There were many complaints from the line's operators, the C&B, about the state of the track and stations and the condition of the only significant structure on the line, the viaduct at Farrangalway. Traders in Kinsale in turn complained about the poor service provided on the line. Two trains each way per day seemed to be the norm for many years, with inconvenient connections at the Junction. Much of the fish traffic from the port continued to go to market in Cork either by sea or road despite the hopes that the railway would be a boon to the fisheries. This first addition to the railway network to the south and west of Cork city was clearly far from a resounding success, with the C&KJR tottering on the brink of insolvency for most of its independent existence.

The initiative to extend the railway west of Bandon did not come from the C&B but from another independent company. Whilst on the whole one can only admire the fortitude and determination of most nineteenth-century Irish railway promoters as they struggled to raise money to extend the iron road into their districts in the face of difficult economic circumstances, there are instances where the historians of these enterprises have to face up to the fact that sometimes these promoters made a bit of a hash of it. I think this charge can be applied to the management of the West Cork Railway which was incorporated in its Act of 1860 to raise capital of £200,000, with additional borrowing powers of up to £66,600 to build a railway the 33 miles from Bandon to Skibbereen. The C&B was supportive, offering to work the new line and undertaking to subscribe £20,000 towards it, but matters got off to a bad start when the contractor appointed was declared bankrupt in 1861 before he could do any work. The ceremonial cutting of the first sod did not take place until May 1863 and then it was decided to start the construction from both ends rather than concentrate on driving the line forward from the existing railhead at Bandon. It was not until June 1866 that the 17 miles from Bandon to Dunmanway were complete and ready for traffic. A further four miles east from Skibbereen were also completed by this time but of course isolated from the rest of the railway. It would be eleven years before this gap was closed.

The C&B reneged on its promise of a contribution of £20,000 to the WCR and possibly because of this the original offer from the C&B to work the new line was declined. The West Cork company decided to run its own trains and began to acquire locomotives and rolling stock. Given the poor state of the WCR's finances this was probably unwise, and as early as April 1866 a writ was received from the carriage and wagon building firm Brown, Marshall & Company seeking payment for rolling stock already supplied. Writs from creditors continued to appear at regular intervals and at one point in 1867 it looked as if the locomotives and rolling stock would have to be sold off and the line closed. The turbulent finances of the WCR finally reached some sort of stability in 1872 when a settlement was reached with its creditors in the Court of Chancery which allowed the company to raise a further £246,000 in preference stock, enabling it to clear off its many outstanding debts.

Perhaps the oddest thing about the WCR was the incredibly inept arrangements it made to handle through traffic at Bandon. As the new line approached the existing C&B route, it ran parallel to the C&B station but at a higher level, so a separate WCR station had to be provided. The two lines were linked east of the WCR passenger station at a spot known as West Cork Junction. However, the WCR dealt with its goods traffic at a separate location to the west of its passenger station. Wagons containing goods for onwards transit were left at a siding at the junction to be collected by the C&B. At first passengers at least had only a short walk between the two stations but then in 1874 the WCR opened a new station called Bandon West about half a mile from the C&B station where it already handled its goods traffic. This meant that through passengers, weighed down with their luggage, had to trudge through the streets of Bandon to and from the new WCR station. This unsatisfactory situation continued until 1880 when the companies amalgamated. From that time onwards all goods and passenger services from the WCR line reversed in and out of the original C&B terminus from West Cork Junction. In 1894 a new station with an island platform was built on the through line, close to the site of the original WCR station. The 1849 C&B station continued to be used for the town's goods traffic until the line closed.

With the line to Dunmanway open, thoughts turned to further extensions. The obvious one was to Skibbereen, linking the existing line to those four miles of track that had been left abandoned since the mid-1860s. There was also a desire to extend the line to Bantry. As any additional commitments were beyond the already impecunious WCR, to build the Skibbereen line yet another new company was set up. It was originally known as the Dunmanway & Skibbereen Railway but this had been changed by the time it got its Act in 1872 to the Ilen Valley Railway. Several of its directors were also on the board of the WCR which agreed to assign the partly completed works near Skibbereen to the new company. The IVR was authorised to raise £80,000 in £10 shares and had borrowing powers for another £20,000. Construction work began in 1875 and matters were helped in 1876 with a loan from the Treasury of £40,000. The WCR was engaged to work the line which opened in July 1877. Three separate companies were now involved in the ownership and working of the 54 miles of railway from Albert Quay to Skibbereen, four if you include the Kinsale branch, and talks began between them to consider an amalgamation. From 1 January, the C&B, WCR, IVR and C&KJ came under the control of one management, though the final name for the new concern had to await an Act of 1888 which created the Cork, Bandon & South Coast Railway.

With the line to Skibbereen open, attention was turned to Bantry. The Ilen Valley Railway Bantry Extension Act was passed in 1878, authorising construction of this 12 mile long line. These powers were later transferred to the C&B which actually built the branch. Work began in November 1879 from its junction with the Skibbereen line at Drimoleague. The contract for the line, which included the cost of erecting the station at Bantry, was worth

£105,000 and was awarded to Thomas Dowling who was also a London-based director of the IVR. There was initially only one intermediate station, at Durrus Road. In July 1881 the line to Bantry opened for both goods and passengers. It terminated at a station high above the town and its harbour, graphically described as Hill Top. In 1892 at the initiative of one of Bantry's most famous (or infamous if you are a student of Irish labour history and in particular the Dublin tram strike of 1913) sons, William Martin Murphy, the line was extended down the hill for two miles to serve new stations at Bantry Town and Bantry Pier.

Having reached Bantry, the railway builders of west Cork were not yet done. There had been agitation for a railway to the sizeable town of Clonakilty since the 1850s. Various schemes had been discussed but none came close to fruition. In 1880 the latest of these was mooted and in August of that year the Clonakilty Extension Railway received parliamentary approval. The C&B made a modest contribution to the new company and agreed to work the line. The branch was 9 miles long and diverged from the former WCR line at Gaggin, a few miles west of Bandon. This was renamed Clonakilty Junction when the line opened in 1886. There was just one intermediate station, Ballinascarthy, which itself was soon to become a junction. This occurred with the opening of yet another new line which diverged there from 1890.

This line was one of many that came in the wake of the passing of the Tramways Act of 1883, the catalyst for a plethora of new railway projects in various parts of Ireland. The Act allowed County Grand Juries, the unelected instruments of local government in Ireland before the advent of the county councils in 1898, to effectively subsidise railway building in their areas. This was done by guaranteeing the interest on the capital used to build the lines by levying a charge on the districts or baronies through which the railway passed and which were deemed to benefit from it. These baronial guarantees were at first restricted to narrow gauge lines and the only broad gauge line built under the terms of the Tramways Act was that which ran from Ballinascarthy to

Courtmacsherry. Various schemes had been suggested over the years to bring a railway to Timoleague, still dominated today by the impressive ruins of a Franciscan abbey dating from 1240 and the nearby seaside village of Courtmacsherry. All of these came to naught but the passing of the Tramways Act and the prospect of baronial guarantees for railway construction which it brought made any railway project, no matter how implausible, providing it had the support of the Grand Jury, much more likely to succeed.

The first plans were for a narrow gauge railway but the line that was eventually built was a broad gauge light railway and roadside tramway. There were actually two separate companies involved in the promotion and building of the 9 miles of track from Ballinascarthy to Courtmacsherry. The first of these was the Ballinascarthy & Timoleague Junction Light Railway. The scheme for the broad gauge line was first announced in 1884 as was notice that the promoters would be asking the Cork Grand Jury to guarantee the company's £25,000 capital at 5 per cent per annum. Nothing happened for another three years when Robert Worthington was awarded the contract to build the line and then in 1888 following further surveys an extension of the line to Courtmacsherry was announced. The extension was to be built by a nominally separate company, the Timoleague & Courtmacsherry Extension Light Railway. The Grand Jury provided baronial guarantees on the £35,000 capital needed to build the entire route and shortly afterwards Worthington began work. It was sensibly suggested at the time that the two companies should be amalgamated but this never happened and they remained separate legal entities up to the time they were taken over by the Great Southern Railways in 1925. The CB&SCR declined to work the new branch so the companies began to acquire their own locomotives and rolling stock to work the line. In the end construction of the line took the best part of two years. Several visits from the Board of Trade inspector's Major-General Hutchinson were required before the first part, the 6 miles from Ballinascarthy to Timoleague, was opened in December 1890. The final stretch to Courtmacsherry did not see traffic until May the following year. One addition was made in 1893 when the line was extended a short distance to the pier at Courtmacsherry.

Only one further extension was now required to complete west Cork's railway network. When one looks back to the struggles to raise money which had dogged railway building in the county almost right from the start, things had certainly changed radically for the better by the time the Baltimore Extension Railway Company was incorporated in 1888 to continue the IVR line, which terminated at Skibbereen, the 9 miles to the fishing port of Baltimore. The building of railways was now a major part of the new economic strategy pursued by the government to improve conditions in the so-called congested districts of the south and west of Ireland. Whereas it had taken the various companies who had promoted the existing lines the best part of 40 years to scrape together the funds to build these, of the estimated £60,000 cost of the BER, £56,700 was given to the company in the form of a grant from the Treasury. The CB&SCR agreed to work the line, which opened in May 1893. There was just one intermediate station, at Creagh. Once the railway was open, there was much discussion about the need for a new pier at Baltimore to encourage the fishing industry. The pier was not in the end built until 1917. At that time, the railway was extended about half a mile from Baltimore station to the pier. Those rails were the most southerly in all of Ireland.

It had taken from 1849 until 1893 to open the 95 route miles (which included the light railway from Ballinascarthy to Courtmacsherry) operated by the CB&SCR. Until 1912 these west Cork lines were isolated from the rest of the Irish railway network. Up to that time the CB&SCR terminus on Albert Quay was one of five stations in Cork city, none of which were linked to each other. In particular, the lack of a connection to the GS&WR station at Glanmire Road, whilst a nuisance for passengers, was a major impediment to goods traffic. It had been hoped that the extension of the railway to places like Kinsale, Bantry and

Baltimore would have aided the development of the fishing industry along the south coast, but for that fish to reach markets outside County Cork it had to be taken across the city on horse drawn carts to the GS&WR station for onward transit.

As part of the development of the new sea route from Rosslare to Fishguard, in 1906 an Act was passed which authorised the Cork City Railways. In October of that year the *Railway Magazine* reported that it was planned to work the line by electric traction, with the current being supplied by the Cork City Tramways and Lighting Company. Unfortunately this interesting idea, which would have seen Ireland's first electrified railway over 70 years before the DART around Dublin, was not pursued. The line was largely paid for by the English Great Western Railway, the driving force behind the Rosslare to Fishguard route and the railway which connected the Irish port to Wexford and Cork. It opened in 1912, was less than a mile long and had a 5mph speed limit. It snaked through the streets of the city from Glanmire Road over two lifting bridges across branches of the River Lee, to Albert Quay. There was never a regular passenger service on the line, though it was used by the occasional excursion train. The route was used to transfer goods traffic originating from the west Cork lines and remained in place until the 1970s. The distinctive girder bridges over the Lee are still to be seen. Rebuilt as fixed bridges in the 1980s, they now carry only road traffic.

The building of a railway network for west Cork occurred during an era when the population of the whole county more than halved in the space of 60 years, from around 854,000 at the time of the 1841 census to less than 405,000 in 1901. This melancholy pattern was evident throughout the whole country, a lasting legacy of the Great Famine, and helps to explain why so many companies struggled to raise the money to build their lines. Lines built to serve predominantly agricultural districts with no industry to speak of or significant mineral traffic in this bruised post-Famine Ireland were not likely to be great investments for their stock holders. Against this unpromising background, the

C&B, and its successor the CB&SCR, did what it could to develop its traffic.

In 1876 a tramway, 880 yards long, was built south of the line from West Cork Junction at Bandon to Allman's distillery and from 1912 another siding diverged just to the west of the same junction, crossing the Bandon River on its own bridge to serve the bottling plant of the brewers Beamish & Crawford. From 1901 to 1913 a 3½ mile long aerial ropeway connected Ballinhassig station with a brickworks at Ballinphelic. A siding was provided to serve a mill near Desert station and on the Clonakilty branch two miles south of Ballinascarthy a branch diverged to serve the Cork Milling Company's flour mill at Shannonvale. This siding opened in 1887 and from then on was the preserve of horse power. Though the Shannonvale Mill branch never carried passengers, unlike its more famous horse-powered counterpart in County Tyrone, the branch from Fintona Junction to Fintona, the line and its final equine locomotive, a grey named *Paddy*, remained in use until the system closed in 1961. Much later, in 1920, a siding was built from the yard at Albert Quay along Victoria Quay to serve the new Ford factory in the city. Despite the efforts to promote the fishing industry on the south coast towards the end of the nineteenth century there was never a large flow of fish traffic along the railways of west Cork. By 1927 it was estimated that only about 2,500 tons of fish were being carried annually. As early as May 1899, in an exchange in the House of Commons between Gerald Balfour and a Dublin member of parliament, the Chief Secretary admitted that of the 47,000 tons of fish landed at Irish ports the previous year, only 14,346 tons were carried by rail, it being cheaper to use coastal shipping than the railways. This was the second of the Balfours to serve as Chief Secretary for Ireland—the younger brother of Arthur, Gerald held the post from 1895 to 1900.

The Post Office was using the railway for the conveyance of mail by the 1860s and for many decades a mail train left Cork very early in the morning. In 1867 this train, which omitted some stops, left Albert Quay at 2.25am. It was still running in more or less the same slot in the summer of 1900 though it had been brought forward to 3.30am. The Mail arrived in Bantry at 6.19am and there was a connection from Drimoleague to Baltimore. The pattern of services offered by the CB&SCR was far from intensive. Staying with the summer timetable of 1900 as an example, after the Mail, there were only five other departures from Albert Quay all day, the last, which only ran as far as Bandon, leaving at 6.00pm. There were four trains in each direction to and from both Bantry and Baltimore, though there were only three round trips on the Clonakilty branch. Two trains each way were deemed sufficient for the traffic on offer on the Timoleague and Courtmacsherry line.

By the end of the nineteenth century more and more tourists from England and further afield were venturing into the remoter parts of the Celtic fringes of the British Isles. Thackeray who, as we saw earlier, did much to promote the scenic attractions of the Glens of Antrim also waxed lyrical about Cork and Kerry and in particular the undoubtedly picturesque area around Glengarriff. A visit by the Prince of Wales to Killarney in 1858 did much to put it on the tourist map. The CB&SCR made great efforts to promote the scenic attractions of west Cork and Kerry to tourists. During the summer, most trains at Bantry were met by tourist cars which ran to Glengarriff and there were also advertised connections to Kenmare and Killarney. Using the CB&SCR, especially after the Kenmare and Valentia branches of the GS&WR had been fully opened in 1893, to reach the Ring of Kerry and Killarney would indeed have involved a journey via a scenic route in both the literal and colloquial senses of the words. In those days of innocence before revolutionary fervour swept the land, when to be called a West Briton was not necessarily a term of abuse, the CB&SCR promoted its circuitous trek to Killarney through west Cork by train and horse-drawn car as the 'Prince of Wales Route'.

On 28 June 1914 in faraway Sarajevo, when Gavrilo Princep and his inept fellow assassins managed, despite themselves after several bungled attempts, to kill the heir to the Austro-Hungarian empire the Archduke Franz Ferdinand, the consequences of their actions were to be shattering for all of Europe. Nothing would ever be the same again as the ripples from the shock wave that followed swept across the continent and eventually even through the island on its western edge. The first great alarm of these troubled times for the citizens of west Cork came the following year when the eyes of the world turned to the waters off the Old Head of Kinsale where on 7 May the *Lusitania* was torpedoed by a German U-boat and sank with the loss of over 1,000 lives. However, it was not so much external events as internal convulsions which were to cause turmoil in Ireland. The 1916 rebellion and its aftermath led to relatively little disruption for the railways apart from those directly affected by the fighting in Dublin. The early years of the war brought an increase in military traffic to and from garrison towns across the country and many new training camps were established to cope with the huge numbers of men who had volunteered in the early months of the war. The railways in Britain had been brought under government control in August 1914 but it was not until the start of 1917 that the same fate befell the Irish companies.

By the time the government relinquished control of the railways in August 1921, many of the companies were already facing an uncertain future. During the war prices and wages had risen dramatically. The wage bills of the Irish companies had increased between 1914 and 1921 by perhaps a measure of five and during the war an eight-hour day for staff had been introduced. While receipts had increased in the same period, they had not kept up with costs. At the same time as the railways' financial position was worsening, the country was plunged into political turmoil and guerilla warfare in the years between 1919 and 1923. There were a number of incidents involving trains in west Cork during the War of Independence, the most serious being an attack at Upton in February 1921 on a train which was conveying some British soldiers. When the 9.15am train from Cork arrived at the station that morning, it was ambushed by a large party of insurgents. In the gun battle that followed, six soldiers and three IRA men were killed along with three railway workers. This incident has passed into republican hagiography, though nowhere in the obligatory song which celebrates the event or on the memorial near the scene is reference made to the innocent railway men killed that day in the course of just doing their normal jobs.

Much worse was to follow during the Civil War. The desultory catalogue of attacks on railway installations that took place elsewhere in the country was repeated in west Cork, with many signal cabins and some stations damaged or destroyed in arson attacks. The most serious incident on the tracks of the CB&SCR occurred in August 1922 when the Chetwynd viaduct was damaged by explosives. Traffic was suspended and following other attacks on bridges further west staff were put on notice that the whole system would close. Repairs to the viaduct were hampered when workmen's trains were fired on but eventually by February the following year it was reopened, though at first passengers had to walk across on foot which must have been a scary experience for anyone with even a hint of vertigo. By the summer of 1923 services had been restored to all parts of the system and the country began to settle down to a more peaceful existence, but given the changed conditions in which the railways were operating, with high costs, declining revenues and the further burden of repairing the physical damage suffered during the civil war, some reorganisation or restructuring of the way the railways were being run was clearly inevitable.

The new Free State government commissioned the first of what would be many reports into the railways, and while the outright nationalisation favoured by some was not pursued, the government encouraged amalgamation of the existing companies. There had already been some discussions between the GS&WR and the CB&SCR about a possible amalgamation between the two companies, but these were subsumed in wider negotiations which led to the creation of the Great Southern

Railways on 1 January 1925. The new company included, in addition to the GS&WR and the CB&SCR, the D&SER, the MGWR and 22 smaller companies all of whose lines were wholly within the jurisdiction of the Irish Free State.

The GSR inherited a damaged railway network and myriad financial and operational problems. It took up the reins at a time when competition from unregulated private buses and lorries was starting to hit the revenues of the railways. It was a private company, with shareholders, but there was precious little money for either dividends or much-needed investment in its worn-out infrastructure. The interwar period was marked in Ireland by a continuing fall in the population and the effects of the international economic depression which followed in the wake of the Wall Street Crash which were exacerbated in Ireland by a tariff war with Britain in the 1930s. These were bleak years in the new state, and inevitably as the losses on many lines began to rise the question of closures came to the fore. The first part of the west Cork network to go was the Kinsale branch which closed in August 1931. The response of the GSR to the mounting losses on this line had been to reduce the service to one train each way daily in 1929. During GSR days the lines to Clonakilty, Baltimore and Courtmacsherry were all threatened at one time or another with closure, but thankfully they survived.

World War Two brought neutrality to the Free State and a major reduction in coal imports from Britain which had a drastic effect on services as the war dragged on. This was at a time when an equally drastic reduction in oil imports rendered private motoring, temporarily at least, virtually extinct, forcing many more people on to the trains. Fuel shortages laid up most lorries as well, increasing the goods traffic on the railways at a time when they were unable to handle it because of lack of coal. In 1939 there were still three passenger workings daily from Albert Quay and three goods trains. By 1941 this was down to one main line passenger train in each direction daily, with connections to and from the branches, and by the end of that year goods trains ran only three days a week. The nadir of services came between the summer of 1944 and July 1945 when passenger trains ran only on two days a week. The trains that did run often had to stop en route through a lack of steam caused by the very poor quality of the coal, if you could call it coal, which was in the bunkers of the locomotives. Daily services were resumed in 1945, but the winter of 1946/47 was one of the worst since records began and again coal supplies from a freezing Britain were curtailed. The service reverted once again to one train a day for a few months and normal services were not restored until the summer of 1947.

The GSR passed away, unmourned by most, in 1945, to be replaced by CIÉ, at first theoretically a company with shareholders but from 1950 fully state-owned and tasked with the management of public transport services in what became the Irish Republic in 1948. Much has been said and written about CIÉ over the years, of which not a lot would have been terribly complimentary, but its management did the best it could with an old and outdated fleet of steam locomotives and carriages and limited funds for investment in more modern equipment. The CB&SCR had bought its last new steam locomotive in 1920, and while the GSR and CIÉ drafted engines from other parts of the network to Albert Quay, these were as old or older than the indigenous fleet. Regular passenger services on the Courtmacsherry line were suspended due to the fuel shortages in February 1947 and never resumed, though goods and summer excursion trains continued to run throughout the 1950s.

As for the rest of the system, the summer timetable for 1950, in operation from 4 June that year, shows how services had deteriorated since 1939. There was now just one through train a day from Albert Quay to Baltimore. This left at 5.30pm and provided connections to Bantry and Clonakilty. In the other direction, the through train left from Skibbereen which meant that bizarrely, except on Saturdays, it was impossible to travel from Baltimore to Cork by rail in one day, though there were again connections from the Bantry and Clonakilty lines. Even allowing for the lack of prosperity and economic activity in general in west Cork in those times, this was a truly appalling service. Railways have a large fixed cost base. Irrespective of whether you run one train or ten each day over a particular stretch of line, the track still has to be maintained, level crossings and signal boxes must be manned, coaches and locomotives have to serviced. The revenue produced by this pathetic level of service could in no way imaginable prove sufficient to cover the basic running costs of the system. Such a poor service offered in response to increasing losses could only lead to even more losses in the long run.

In fairness to CIÉ, the west Cork lines were modernised in the mid-1950s. In 1952 the company took delivery of a fleet of diesel railcars and some of these were drafted on to the former CB&SCR lines in 1954, taking nearly 40 minutes off the time a steam-hauled train was allowed to make the run from Cork to Bantry. In the summer timetable of 1955 two services were running daily from Cork to Bantry which was now recognised as the main line with connections to the Skibbereen and Clonakilty branches. In 1957, the new C class diesel locomotives were being used on the west Cork lines, mainly on goods trains, but occasionally photographers were able to record these brand new machines at the head of a couple of ancient passenger coaches. Almost all services were now in the hands of diesel traction, with steam being relegated to sugar beet specials and as cover for the failures of the diesels from time to time. With the use of diesel traction and the introduction of additional if still infrequent services, CIÉ at least made an attempt to modernise the system. To put this in context, by 1957 the modernisation plan for British Railways which had been published in 1955 was still in its very early stages and the vast majority of passenger and goods trains across the Irish Sea were being hauled by steam locomotives at this time.

So just as things were starting to look up for the west Cork lines at last, along came Todd Andrews. He took over as head of CIÉ in September 1958 at a time when government policy towards the company was about to undergo a change which saw the long-held aspiration that CIÉ should break even becoming a firm policy objective. The previous year a government-appointed committee headed by Dr J.P. Beddy, whose task was to examine all aspects of internal transport in the state, had published its report. The headline from the Beddy Report as far as the railways were concerned was a suggestion that railway mileage in the Republic be reduced by 65 per cent, with the closure of over 1,000 miles of track. This was remarkably prophetic as the system envisaged by Beddy was very similar to that which exists today. The instrument of execution for mass closures was provided in the Transport Act of 1958 which gave CIÉ a free hand to propose the closure of any line that it did not think was viable. There was subtlety in this on the part of the government as it placed the responsibility for railway closures on CIÉ and kept the politicians at a distance from them. The Act also provided legislative substance to the quest for the Holy Grail in that it guaranteed CIÉ an annual grant of one million pounds until 1964, by which time, through restructuring and mass railway closures, hey presto, operating expenditure would not be greater than CIÉ's revenue. The Grail would then be passed round the boardroom table at Kingsbridge as pigs prepared to take off from runways all over the twenty-six counties.

The new broom began to sweep with alarming speed. Within two months of his appointment, in October 1958, the most notorious closure of the Andrews era, that of the Harcourt Street line from Dublin to Bray, was announced and went ahead in January 1959. Under the 1958 Act, CIÉ was judge, jury and executioner. The company could initiate an investigation into any line that was losing money. The CIÉ board would then discuss a report on that line prepared by its own staff and if it deemed that there was no prospect of the losses being reversed, it would announce the closure. By the summer of 1960, a long list of routes for closure was being prepared which included all the former CB&SCR lines. It was all done with indecent haste, in an almost

Stalinist fashion. TDs and local delegations could huff and puff with all the energy they could muster, for all the good it would do. Petitions against the closures containing thousands of signatures were simply ignored. There was no structure for consultation or to enforce a re-evaluation of a closure proposal; hence Andrews' reluctance to meet the deputation from west Cork mentioned at the start of the chapter. Once the politburo at Kingsbridge had spoken, there was no realistic hope of a reprieve for a line. Despite widespread local opposition, rail services from Albert Quay ended on 31 March 1961.

The one part of the system which lingered on was the Cork City Railways. Albert Quay remained open as a goods depot and goods trains continued to run across the city sporadically into the 1970s. At Glanmire Road, the connection to Albert Quay was from the goods yard just south of the passenger station. Shortly after leaving the yard, for years locomotives routinely steamed past the petrol pumps of a garage at the junction of Alfred Street and Glanmire Road, the stuff of nightmares for today's health and safety industry, before crossing the North Channel of the River Lee on the distinctive girder-built Brian Boru bridge. Usually preceded by a man with a red flag, the train continued crossing over the South Channel on the Clontarf Bridge before entering the yard at the side of the passenger platforms at Albert Quay. Both bridges were designed to be raised to allow boats to pass. The station building on Albert Quay, still in fine external condition, is in use as offices but a modern office block built directly behind it removes any possibility of it ever seeing trains again.

Beyond the confines of the city there are still many reminders of the railways that once served west Cork, none finer than the Chetwynd viaduct which is situated about five miles from the city centre on the road to Bandon. Perched on top of their lofty piers, the four steel arches still stride majestically across the valley, the epitome of Victorian engineering at its best, combining utilitarian purpose with grace and elegance. At Bandon, the high-level through station dating from 1894 is now used by Cork County Council as offices, and across the road some of the buildings from the earlier low-level station, dating from 1849 and used as a goods depot up to closure, can also still be seen. Further west in the district of Gaggin, while road improvements have swept away all traces of Clonakilty Junction, a name board, whether original or a replica I cannot say, but certainly in an appropriate style and typography, marks the site of the junction to any passing motorists who care to take notice.

The trackbed of the former light railway between Timoleague and Courtmacsherry has been converted into a foot and cycle path. Joggers with their i-Pods and ducks preening their plumage may have replaced the steam and diesel locomotives which once trundled along the roadside tramway beside the sea between the two villages with their trains of sugar beet or excited excursionists, but this is still recognisable as a former railway. If only more miles of abandoned railway had been given this treatment what an asset they would be for the country and what a boon for walkers and cyclists. The speed limit on the roadside tramway section of the line was 12mph, which a cyclist on the route today could easily better. A signal of doubtful parentage is located close to the bridge which took the tramway and the road over an inlet of Courtmacsherry Bay close to where the Arigideen River enters the sea. One of the railway's locomotives built in 1894 took its name from the river, but as if to emphasise the problems associated with the spelling of Irish place names it was spelt *Argadeen*. At Courtmacsherry a bi-lingual nameboard in the style of the GSR and an adjacent plaque recall the memory of the tramway.

In Skibbereen the distinctive steel-girder bridge with its span of 112 ft over the River Ilen is still extant. This dated from the opening of the extension to Baltimore in 1893. Some of the sheds in the adjacent station area are still recognisable from old photos of the place in its heyday. However, a hotel blocks the course of the line at the south end of the river bridge, though on the gable of a house, at the site of the level crossing where the line crossed Bridge Street, is a fine mural featuring a very accurate depiction of one of the famous 'Bandon Tanks'. Between 1906 and 1920 eight of these powerful machines, with the 4-6-0 wheel arrangement not often used on tank locomotives, were built by Beyer Peacock in Manchester for the line. Two of these, CIÉ Nos 463 and 464, survived the closure of the Cork lines and were still on the books of the company when steam traction in the Irish Republic officially ended in 1963. A new road has been built on the trackbed of the first part of the line to Baltimore beyond Bridge Street. Baltimore station itself is in good condition and is now the premises of a sailing school. However, there is no trace of the rails on the pier which were once the most southerly in Ireland.

Much has changed in County Cork since the last train left Albert Quay to head west in 1961. The city itself has grown rapidly and yet today there is no alternative for commuters coming in from the south and west but to use the roads. If the lines to Bandon and Kinsale had survived there would surely be a well patronised service of commuter trains on them today using modern railcars similar to the services now offered on the lines to the north and east of the city. Is it fantasy to think of thousands of back packers and tourists also taking the train to Bantry, Skibbereen and Baltimore, had they the option today? I don't think so and it just goes to show how so much in life is transient and how the decisions which one generation thinks make good sense are shown to be shortsighted and wrong by the next.

It probably is fantasy to think of the railways of west Cork in anything other than the past tense. It would simply cost too much to rebuild them, and how a link from such a revived line could be made to Kent station at Glanmire Road on the other side of the city centre is certainly beyond me. I doubt if the present city fathers would tolerate trains rolling through the streets of their city on the route of the Cork City Railways with or without a factotum leading the procession waving a red flag. Oil is still relatively cheap and plentiful but I suppose you never know what is round the corner. There may come a time when it does become a realistic proposition to reinstate at least some of these lines, though for the foreseeable future the Chetwynd viaduct must remain as an object d'art, a sculpture honouring the memory of its builders rather than part of the major transport artery it once was.

Chapter 7 ❧

| MR BALFOUR GOES WEST

Arthur Balfour was a remarkable man whose career has had, indirectly, a profound and long-lasting impact on the whole world into the first decade of the new millennium. This stems from his most famous incursion into history in the form of the Balfour Declaration. Deeply religious all his life, there was something of the Old Testament in him, and at a time when many of his class romanticised the Arab world he had a theological empathy for the Jewish people, sharing the Zionist perspective that they should be restored to their traditional biblical homeland. As Foreign Secretary in 1917 at the height of the First World War, anxious along with Prime Minister Lloyd George to secure the support of Jews around the world for the war effort, Balfour wrote to Lord Rothschild, a leading temporal figure in the Jewish community in Britain. In that letter he gave official British encouragement to the formation of a Jewish state in Palestine from which in 1917 British forces were engaged in dislodging its Ottoman Turkish rulers. He was not to know it at the time, nor did anyone else, but this proved to be one of the turning points in the history of the last century, about which indirectly we are all reminded every time we check in at an airport today. However, long before this, in another world, at the height of Pax Britannica, a conceit which paradoxically even the most enthusiastic of Victorian imperialists would have struggled at the time to apply to Britain's closest neighbour, Balfour, when he was serving as Chief Secretary for Ireland, made another sort of impact, part of which forms the subject of this chapter.

This is a book about long closed and half remembered railways in different parts of the country and not about politics. However, the last great phase of railway construction in Ireland owed as much to politics as anything else, so it is impossible to examine this part of the history of Ireland's railways and in particular some of the lines that are featured in this book without including an examination of that political dimension in some detail. Apart from the subject of this chapter, the line from Westport to Achill which we will get to in due course, the routes explored in the next two chapters were also built around the same time and owe their existence to the same political dynamic. In the 1890s there were two reasons why Conservative politicians at Westminster were keen to subsidise the building of railways in the south and west of Ireland in those areas which would shortly become known as the congested districts. There was a genuine desire to improve economic conditions in those areas and ease the dire poverty of many of the inhabitants. However, it was also hoped that as the wealth of these districts increased the demand for a parliament in Dublin would be diluted. This policy has come to be known as constructive unionism or, in a phrase used by Gerald Balfour, who followed his brother and served as Chief Secretary for Ireland from 1895 to 1900, in a letter to one of his constituents in Leeds, it was an attempt to kill Home Rule with kindness.

Arthur Balfour was a politician for most of his adult life, eventually becoming Prime Minister, serving in that office from July 1903 to December 1905. On the face of it, given his background this was hardly surprising. He was born in 1848 in East Lothian in Scotland into a political family. His father was a Tory MP and his mother was a member of the Cecil dynasty who would provide a Tory Prime Minister in the form of the Marquis of Salisbury in the 1880s. Despite this, Balfour seems initially at least to have been a reluctant politician, much more at ease as an academic and a philosopher. He entered parliament in 1874 and when his uncle became Prime Minster he first served in a couple of junior posts before being appointed Chief Secretary for Ireland with a seat in the cabinet in 1887. The explanation for this meteoric rise to prominence is said to have given us the phrase 'Bob's your uncle'. In the course of the nineteenth century, with the absence of any parliament in Ireland, the role of Chief Secretary had risen in importance. It was the closest thing the country had to a chief executive or a Prime Minister, albeit one unelected by the people over whom he presided. Even though in this case nepotism literally may have played a part in Balfour getting the job, it was far from a sinecure for he was put in charge of a country that was virtually at war with itself.

The dark shadow of the Great Famine still hung ominously over the whole country four decades on from its immediate and devastating effects. The population was still in decline, large swathes of each new generation became emigrants, there was little prosperity and there were sporadic local famines in the west. Anger over British inaction at the time and in the aftermath of the Great Famine had spilled over into a revival of the physical force tradition of politics. Essentially this amounted to nothing more than futile gestures inviting coercion and achieving little beyond the odd spectacular or glorious failure. The distant government in London made little effort to address the key issue of land ownership which led to the suppurating sore of evictions, agrarian violence and boycotts that had exploded into the Land War by the 1870s. At the same time and linked to these essentially economic issues was the growing demand for Home Rule which a majority of the ruling class in Britain refused to countenance under any circumstances.

The demand for Irish Home Rule was at the very centre of British politics in the 1880s. The 1885 election returned a block of 86 Irish Nationalist MPs under the disciplined leadership of Parnell. Gladstone's Liberals, though the largest party overall, were dependent on the support of the Irish Nationalists to form a government. Gladstone, the Liberal prime minister, was a supporter of Home Rule but the bill he introduced to bring this about was defeated in 1886, splitting his party in the process. The election which followed brought Balfour's uncle to power, leading a minority Tory government dependent on Liberal Unionist support. Back in Ireland dismay at the failure to win a parliament in Dublin was replaced by a determination to pursue with renewed vigour the other key element in Nationalist demands, land reform. The 1886 Plan of Campaign backed by the Irish Parliamentary Party continued the work of the Land League in organising rents strikes and boycotting those involved in supporting evictions of tenants for non-payment of rents. Ostensibly a non-violent campaign, inevitably it veered towards intimidation and random acts of violence, with frequent clashes between protestors and police reducing large parts of rural Ireland to a state of near anarchy. This was the poisoned chalice which Bob had handed to his nephew.

There was disbelief at the appointment among many at Westminster. Balfour was perceived as a dilettante, an inexperienced lightweight. Some were concerned that his health would not be up to the rigours of the job and the regular journeys of 12 hours or more in duration which he had to make to get to and from Ireland. He was no great orator (one commentator referred to him as 'a lisping Hawthorn bird'), and he was pitted against some tough and experienced bruisers on the Irish side in Parnell, Tim Healy and others. Balfour was subjected to almost daily tirades in the House of Commons as Nationalist MPs railed against each new example of police brutality or enforced evictions. But the Chief Secretary had very clear views from the outset on how to deal with the Irish problem. He believed that poverty, not politics, was the key to the resolution of the issue and that if a measure of prosperity could be provided for the Irish peasantry then political agitation would die away. It was a bold strategy and it was not without intellectual merit. The problem was that he believed that before measures could be taken to improve economic conditions on the ground, law and order had to be restored. There could be no prosperity while agrarian disorder and outrages, as he saw them, were taking place.

Balfour's means to restore order was a coercion bill, the Irish Crimes Act of 1887. This abolished trial by jury for cases dealing with agrarian disorder and boycotting, the accused being brought before two stipendiary magistrates instead. Hundreds were imprisoned under the Act, including at one time six Irish MPs who were jailed for making seditious speeches.

Balfour was transformed in the eyes of many in Ireland virtually overnight, from a lisping fop to 'bloody Balfour'. The Dublin newspaper the *Freeman's Journal* called him 'the meanest mortal who has ever directed the policy of the English government in Ireland'. Balfour himself did little to calm the opposition to his policy of coercion. In one badly judged response to the question as to how he expected to succeed in resolving the Irish problem when so many before him had failed, he replied: 'Cromwell failed because he relied solely on repressive measures. That mistake I shall not imitate. I shall be as relentless as Cromwell in enforcing obedience to the law, but, at the same time, I shall be as radical as any reformer in redressing grievances and especially in removing every cause of complaint in regards to the land. Hitherto, English governments have stood first on one leg and then upon the other. They have either been all for oppression or all for reform. I am for both; repression as stern as Cromwell: reform as thorough as Mr Parnell or anyone else can desire.' The reference to Cromwell had a predictably hostile reaction but this response is constructive unionism in a nutshell, the wielding of the stick followed by an abundance of carrots. It was only five years since another Chief Secretary, Lord Frederick Cavendish, had been murdered in the Phoenix Park by the Invincibles, a splinter group of the Irish Republican Brotherhood, so the current Chief Secretary had to be accompanied by two armed detectives on all his travels at this time.

Balfour's Crimes Act had a term of three years and it seemed to be working. Even as the stick was being waved, the other part of his policy towards Ireland was manifesting itself. A new Land Act in 1887 extended the terms of Gladstone's Land Act of 1881 to include leaseholders. Another Land Act passed the next year added £5 million to the funds available under the Ashbourne Land Purchase Act of 1885, and the Irish Land Purchase Act of 1891 had provision for sums of up to the region of £30 million to be made available to allow tenants to purchase their land from their landlords. Under this Act most tenants were actually paying less towards buying their land over a 50-year term than they had previously been paying annually in rent. Balfour did not originate the idea of land purchase schemes but he greatly accelerated the process and in doing so he helped to create the huge class of small peasant proprietors who dominated the economic life of rural Ireland in the century that followed. In May 1892 John Redmond, later to be the leader of the Irish Party when a Home Rule Act was finally given Royal Assent in September 1914, wrote, 'It must be acknowledged that the Land Act of last year is a great measure and on my part I do not grudge Mr Balfour any praise he may be entitled to.' Even his bitter political opponents had to recognise his major contribution to finally resolving this problem which had debilitated Ireland for decades.

While correctly identifying the land issue as being at the core of the problems of the country, the other thrust of Balfour's policy was in the area of economic development and his most significant measure here was the establishment of the Congested Districts Board in 1891. Over the next 30 years the Board actively assisted the building of roads, bridges and piers in those counties from Donegal to Cork that were deemed to be congested, a term which linked to their rateable value rather than population density, best translated in this context as meaning impoverished. The Board was active in introducing measures to improve agriculture and fisheries, but ultimately its main contribution to the areas it served was once again in facilitating land purchase schemes. The other measure deemed to advance economic development was the passing in 1889 of the Light Railways (Ireland) Act, the first of two pieces of legislation which over the next decade were to finance the building of many miles of railways in the south and west of Ireland. The 1889 Act, often referred to as the Balfour Act, allowed the government to make grants to build lines in areas where it would have been difficult to raise the capital required and simplified the procedures involved in the promotion of such schemes.

This Act and the focus on railways as a means of economic regeneration had their origins not with Balfour himself but in the report of the Allport Commission. This body was appointed by the government in 1885 to investigate the conduct of public works in Ireland. It chairman was Sir James Allport who had been general manager of the English Midland Railway for many years and was one of the most respected railway executives in the country. Allport's main claim to fame was his policy of providing cheap and comfortable travel for Third Class passengers on the MR at a fare of one penny per mile. Most of the other railway companies followed his lead and the lot of the poorer passenger was greatly improved in the course of time. The Allport Commission's report which was published in 1888 recommended the building of eleven railways in what would soon be known as the congested districts, some of which were eventually built. More significantly, the Commission endorsed the principle of direct state funding to build lines which were desirable for reasons of economic development and it was this recommendation which found legislative expression in the Balfour Act and in a later Act of 1896.

Coercion was by its very nature a quicker acting solution than economic development. While there may have been a certain war weariness in rural Ireland by the end of the 1880s, Balfour had a stroke of luck which greatly helped to further his political objectives when Parnell was found to be in *flagranto delicto* with Mrs Kathleen O'Shea, the estranged wife of a fellow MP. His subsequent citing in her divorce led to a split in his party as the smack of croziers hitting the ground in moral indignation reverberated all over Ireland. Even louder was the tut-tutting coming from Parnell's Liberal allies at Westminster whose strong non-conformist traditions were offended by his involvement in the divorce case. With the once highly focused and disciplined Irish Nationalist party in disarray and any prospect of Home Rule receding into the distance, Arthur Balfour probably thought this time was as good as any to make a tour of the congested districts which he was trying to propel towards prosperity.

The Chief Secretary set out from Dublin on 26 October 1890 accompanied by his sister, the Under Secretary for Ireland Sir West-Ridgway and two private secretaries. The weather was inclement most of the time and the party travelled by train, by horse-drawn car and on foot. Balfour broke a finger early on the trip as he tried to close the window in a car in which he was travelling and was in some discomfort throughout. They visited most of the counties where the congested districts were located, from Donegal in the north through Mayo and Galway to Kerry in the south. He attended meetings with local people and their leaders and met many delegations. In Dungloe the meeting discussed public works and possible railways in the area. Perhaps this was the genesis of the line discussed in the next chapter though that was to be delivered by the other Balfour, Gerald, who was Chief Secretary for Ireland from 1896 to 1900. Much to the chagrin of Nationalist politicians, Balfour was well received wherever he went both by the people and, as significantly, by their priests. The Nationalist MP Willie Redmond had a singular explanation for his cordial reception in County Mayo. Addressing a National League meeting in Dublin he said, 'Mr Balfour's tour is one of the meanest of his acts. He dare not go to face the men of Mayo without his sister, for he knew no matter in what light they regarded him, they would not do anything discourteous to a lady.'

Balfour seems to have been shocked to the core by the poverty and degradation which he found on his tour. One of his biographers described his visit to the village of Doogla on Achill island which was described as no more than a collection of mud huts. There was a half-finished bridge over some swampy ground dividing this from the next habitation which Balfour offered to pay to have completed out of his own money. Giving an account of his tour in a speech in Liverpool the next month he spoke of an experience in south Donegal where he walked between hovels watching the people digging out black and half rotten potatoes and seeing wretched twice-shorn sheep trying to survive on the poor pastures that surrounded the people's homes. This was his first-hand account of the partial failure of the potato crop in the winter of 1890/91, though this time effective relief measures were put in place and its effects were nowhere near as devastating as had occurred in the 1840s. The events of 1890/91 however highlight how little had really changed in the west in the half century following the Great Famine.

Before Balfour's visit there was already much discussion about building further railways in County Mayo. The Allport Commission had taken evidence in favour of several additional lines in the county. Two of these proposals were centred on Ballina. One was for a line from there inland via Crossmolina to Belmullet on the shores of Blacksod Bay. The other was for a shorter line north from Ballina to Killala. This line was eventually built with assistance from the government under the terms of the Balfour Act, the 8 mile long branch from Ballina to Killala opening in January 1893. The Commission also discussed a line from Westport to Newport and Mallaranny where it would terminate. There was no talk at this stage of going on towards Achill.

Any lines in Mayo required the co-operation of the only railway company active in the area, the Midland Great Western. Approaches were made to the MGWR as early as February 1890 to work both the proposed lines in Mayo and a third Balfour line, that from Galway to Clifden. By September agreement had been reached between the company and the government to construct, maintain and operate the three lines. This announcement in the railway press followed a meeting the previous month between Sir Ralph Cussack, the Chairman of the Midland Great Western Railway, and Balfour. Even at this late stage there was still no suggestion that the line from Westport should go any further than Mallaranny. The decision to extend the line to the shores of Achill Sound was probably made by Balfour himself during his tour of October 1890. He had clearly been moved by the desperate poverty he had witnessed for himself on the island and was impressed by the arguments put forward by a deputation of local dignitaries led by their parish priest that the line should be extended. The way the line was eventually constructed, in two sections, suggests that the plans for the Westport to Mallaranny line were already well advanced, with the extension to Achill being bolted on, almost certainly because of the direct intervention of the Chief Secretary himself.

The plans for the first part of the line were approved by the County Mayo Grand Jury in November 1890. The contract for the Westport to Mallaranny line, worth £110,000, was awarded to Robert Worthington and work began in December 1890. The contract had stipulated that the line should be completed in two years but by the end of 1892 it was nowhere near ready. There were many disagreements between the MGWR and Barrington, Worthington's engineer, and the final location of Mallaranny station had not even been determined at that time due to apparent indecision about the course of the line from there to Achill. An extension of 18 months was granted to Worthington to complete the works but a further problem arose in September 1893 when he declared himself to be bankrupt. The MGWR had to take over the works on the unfinished line. Eventually in January 1894, Major General Hutchinson of the Board of Trade was invited to inspect the line from Westport to Newport which finally opened for traffic from 1 February 1894. The remaining part of the first section of the Achill line from Newport to Mallaranny opened to the public from 16 July of that year, but before services commenced one particular special train ran in the most tragic of circumstances which are related below.

The second part of the line from Mallaranny to Achill was built under the auspices of a separate company, the Achill Extension

Railway Company. The cost of the 8¼ mile line was to be in the region of £56,000. The scheme was approved by the county's Grand Jury in July 1891. The line from Westport to Mallaranny had been built by the MGWR using government money but the extension was constructed by the Board of Works. Despite numerous requests from the Board, the MGWR refused to enter into any agreement to work the extension until it had been completed to their satisfaction. The work had progressed sufficiently for a Board of Trade inspection in March 1895. Another followed in May when approval was given for public services to commence, with the first train running the full 27 mile length of the line from Westport to Achill on the 13th of that month. There were several significant engineering features on the line. There were viaducts at Westport and Newport and its two admittedly short tunnels were the only ones on the whole MGWR system. In addition much of the line was steeply graded. It had many stretches where the gradient was as severe as 1 in 60 or 1 in 70.

When the first part of the line opened from Westport to Newport in February 1894, a service of two trains each day, one in the morning and one in the afternoon, was provided. As the line was extended first to Mallaranny and then to Achill, this meagre level of service was continued. In summer a third train was sometimes scheduled. The pattern of services established in those early years continued for most of the line's existence. In its early years, the first train for Achill sometimes started from Castlerea, though in later years locomotives and crews for the branch were provided by the engine shed at Westport. For example, in 1900 the first train due into Achill at 11.30am had started from Castlerea at 7.35am that morning. This service called at Manulla Junction where it provided a connection to the line to Ballina and Killala. After calling at Castlebar it arrived at Westport at 9.28am, leaving for Achill at 9.40am. In that year, a First Class single from Dublin to Achill cost 35 shillings and one penny and a Third Class return ticket would have set the traveller back 29 shillings and five pence.

Throughout the existence of the Achill branch there was a through connection from Dublin in the morning, with a coach for Achill attached to the *Limited Mail* which usually left the Broadstone between 7 and 7.30am. This took about seven hours to reach its westerly destination. There was also a connection to this service from Kingstown and the overnight steamer from Holyhead. In the summer timetable for 1900 the *Limited Mail* left Dublin at 7.00am. The distance covered by this coach was 187 miles, providing one of the longest through runs in Ireland. The only regular timetabled service which exceeded this was that from Kingsbridge to Tralee, though briefly in the early 1950s, when the GNR's *Enterprise Express* from Belfast to Dublin was extended for a few years to run through to Cork, this trumped both of these. A copy of the MGWR working timetable dating from January 1920—this was the one used by railway staff as opposed to that issued to the public—shows the *Limited Mail* now left Dublin at 7.25am. Passengers using this service did not reach Achill until 2.18pm in the afternoon. In that year there were still three trains on the branch, with the early one, which left Westport at 8.00am, running as a mixed train conveying goods wagons as well as passenger coaches. This meant that any passengers had to kick their heels for 15 minutes at both Newport and Mallaranny as the engine went off to shunt the goods wagons it had brought into the sidings there for unloading.

At first, small E class six-wheeled tank engines were used to work the trains on the Achill branch. These were later replaced by a type of small 4-4-0 tender locomotive. Originally built as 2-4-0s by Beyer Peacock in 1880/81, these were rebuilt by the MGWR at Broadstone to become the company's first 4-4-0s. These engines were associated with the line for such a long time they were given the nickname of the Achill bogies. By way of complete contrast to these conventional steam locomotives, in 1912 the MGWR tried out a very early petrol-engined railcar on the line, the first such vehicle ever to run in Ireland and probably one of the first in all of Europe. The company had introduced this for the carriage of mails but it also had accommodation for some passengers. The railcar was not a success in its original form but it survived into the GSR era as an inspection car with the company's Engineers Department.

One of the obvious consequences of the extreme poverty that assailed the west of Ireland was emigration which caused the population of counties such as Mayo to decline from the 1850s well into the second half of the twentieth century. But almost as debilitating was the regular migration of thousands of young and active people to do seasonal agricultural work in Britain. Some of these migrants became emigrants in time but many came back to work on the family farm or small holding for the rest of the year. It was a sad reflection on the lack of work in their own districts and the meagre incomes they could scrape from their own bits of land that many were forced to make these long treks to England and Scotland every year to earn the extra money that helped to prevent their families from starving. On the morning of 16 June 1894, several hundred Achill people boarded a hooker which would take them to Westport Quay where they would join a steamer bound for Glasgow to work on the potato harvest in Scotland. All went well until the hooker was in sight of Westport Quay when it capsized. Some reports blame the crew for trimming the sails at the wrong time. Others suggest that it was a surge of passengers to one side of the hooker to look at the steamer they were later to board that caused the craft to capsize. A total of 32 of its passengers were drowned, 25 of whom were girls. The youngest was only 12 years old. A special train was organised to bring home the remains of those who had perished in the tragedy. It was hauled beyond Newport by one of the contractors' locomotives on the part of the line that was not yet open for public service.

The opening of the line was marked by a tragedy, as was its closing, and it is impossible to write about the railway to Achill without mentioning the prophesy that is believed by some to have foretold both events. Four decades might have elapsed since the line opened but young people from Achill still migrated to Scotland to help with the harvest. On the night of 13 September 1937 near Kirkintilloch in Lanarkshire a bothy in which a number of boys from Achill were sleeping caught fire. The doors of the bothy were locked and ten boys aged between 10 and 23 perished in the conflagration. Final closure plans for the line had already been announced, with the order putting these into effect being signed by the Free State Minister of Industry and Commerce John Leydon on the 24th of that month. A special train brought the coffins of the deceased and their grieving relatives back to Achill in a terrible echo of the tragedy that had marked the opening of the line in 1894. The bodies of the victims of the Kirkintilloch fire were laid to rest in the graveyard at Kildamhnait, or Kildownet as it is sometimes spelt, on the south-east coast of the island. Their memorial is close to that of the victims of the 1894 tragedy in the same cemetery.

Some people are disposed to believe in prophesy, making much of the enigmatic verses of Nostradamus which can be interpreted in many ways to mean many things. In this case the prophet concerned was Brian Rua O' Cearbhain who lived on Achill in the seventeenth century. This seer prophesied that carts on iron wheels emitting smoke and fire would carry bodies into Achill on their first and last journeys. Make of that what you will but this story will always be linked to the line and aftermath of the two terrible events which marked the beginning and the conclusion of its story.

When Arthur Balfour spoke about his visit to the west of Ireland one theme that recurs is the contrast he found between the natural beauty of the landscape and the desperate poverty of its inhabitants. The Victorians invented tourism as we know it in these islands. What is widely believed to be the world's first excursion train predated even the *Irish Mail*. It ran from Leicester to Loughborough in July 1841, organised by a certain Mr Thomas Cook to take a band of campaigners to a temperance meeting— no chance of a jar on that special then. Tourism blossomed almost organically with the development of the railway network which provided a means for the curious and the rich to explore the remoter parts of their own country. As the middle classes grew both in wealth and in numbers throughout the nineteenth century, they espoused with enthusiasm the idea of taking holidays, and as the century progressed they were prepared to venture further afield.

The railways built under the Balfour Act and the Railways (Ireland) Act of 1896 were essentially a means of encouraging economic development. One perhaps surprisingly modern element in this was a conscious attempt to use the railways to develop tourism in the areas they served. A little known aspect of the 1896 Act was that it allowed the government, through the Board of Works, to provide subsidies for steamer and road services in the congested districts largely for the benefit of summer visitors. Belmullet may have missed out on a railway in the 1890s but it had a regular steamer service from Sligo, sponsored by the Board of Works. In 1900 this ran three times a week from May to September and twice weekly for the rest of the year. There were other services on offer such as a coach from Listowel to Tarbert to connect with steamers on the Shannon estuary, some of which called at Cappagh Pier near Kilrush from where an onwards connection was available to Kilkee via the West Clare Railway. A great deal of effort was made by many Irish railway companies in the late nineteenth century to promote the tourist trade and encourage visitors from Britain. There was even an Irish Railways Tourist Office at Charing Cross in London for a time selling travel tickets and making hotel reservations. The MGWR was a leading player and made determined efforts to exploit the tourist potential of its new lines in the west.

The company was an early entrant into the hotel business, opening an establishment in Galway beside its station in Eyre Square in the 1850s. With the completion of the lines to Clifden and Achill the company decided to build hotels close to both lines, at Recess on the line into Connemara and Mallaranny on the Achill branch. In 1895 the company bought over 50 acres of land bordered by the railway near the village and in July of that year a contract was issued for the building of the hotel which opened its doors to its first guests in the summer of 1896. It was set in a picturesque location close to Clew Bay and was equipped with all the modern conveniences of that era including electric lighting in all its rooms which must have been a great novelty at the time, certainly in Mayo. A golf course was laid out on the adjoining land at the turn of the century and the hotel also offered hot and cold sea water baths—an almost mandatory, if to our eyes puzzling, feature of the late Victorian holiday experience. Combined rail and hotel tickets were issued from 1898 and such was the success of the hotel it was extended in 1900. The railway company operated or sponsored horse-drawn cars which ran from June to September from Westport to Clifden and from Achill station to Dugort on the island. Cyclists were also encouraged to tour the area, using the hotel as their base. Special rates were available for the carriage of cycles on the trains. In 1900 it cost one shilling to convey a bicycle for 150 miles on MGWR trains.

What the locals, most of whom were still living in conditions which were not far removed from those of the 1840s, made of this oasis of bourgeois luxury in their midst is not recorded in any source I have seen and whether the development of tourism made any significant contribution to the economy of the area is another matter for conjecture. If the demography of County Mayo and the other congested districts is any sort of a guide then the measures taken by the government at the end of the nineteenth century did not succeed as the population continued its inexorable decline and the local economy had not even improved sufficiently to bring an end to the seasonal migrations of many across the Irish Sea to work as agricultural labourers at harvest time in England and Scotland.

Traffic on the Achill branch was severely disrupted during the Civil War. The area around Newport seemed to have been a particular stronghold of the insurgency. Bridges were blown up, locomotives were maliciously derailed and several carriages were destroyed in arson attacks. When the Civil War ended in 1923 and normality was at last restored the next challenge to the old order came with the establishment of the GSR in 1925. The new owners changed the name of the hotel at Mallaranny to the Great Southern, a name it continued to carry long after the eventual demise of the GSR itself in 1945. As has been mentioned elsewhere, these were dark days in the new state and for its principal railway operator. If the two decades before the Great War represent the apogee of the Irish railway network, it did not take long for it to sink from this highpoint in its fortunes. Independence did little to improve the economic condition of the 26 counties and the railways were assailed by ferocious and unregulated competition from private bus and lorry operators. Legislation from 1927 onwards began to catch up with part of this crisis by attempting to regulate bus and road freight services. The international financial and economic crisis which followed in the wake of the Wall Street Crash in 1929 made a bleak picture even bleaker. The state of the roads in that part of Mayo provided some respite for the Achill line and by 1929 the GSR had control of the county's largest bus company, the Irish Omnibus Company, though this did not stop the IOC from running a service from Achill to Westport and Ballina in competition with the trains from 1933.

The legislation which set up the GSR also abolished the baronial guarantees that had subsidised many lines built from the 1880s onwards. The compensation provided by the state in return was inevitably not sufficient to make up the difference. The Balfour lines had been financed by direct grants from the British government and were not even included in the notional compensation for the loss of the baronial guarantees in 1924. In addition to the losses they were making another problem loomed at this time, the state of the railways themselves. The Balfour lines would never have been built without government money. Even though they were unlikely to generate enough profits to allow their track to be renewed, there was no provision in the original legislation for this. The lines were paid for by the government and then handed over to the operating companies but there the capital subsidies ended and by the late 1920s the state of the track was becoming a serious problem. The original rails and sleepers were life expired but there was no money available to replace them. This gave the GSR another reason to look at the economics of lines such as that to Achill, and the Railways Act passed by the Fianna Fáil government in 1933 gave the company a legislative tool which could be used to close unremunerative lines. This was found in section 9 of the Act which allowed the railway company to replace 'a service of trains in respect of which the railway company running such service wishes, for the purposes of more economical working, to provide by means of road transport such transport facilities as are required by the traffic theretofore carried by such service'. This meant that if road services could do the job and were cheaper to run as invariably they were then the railway could be closed. The spate of closures in the Free State in the 1930s was an attempt to improve the poor financial position of the company at that time.

All types of traffic on the Achill line had been in decline for a number of years. One figure quoted by a GSR official suggested it was losing £4,000 per year. In the closure proposals the savings which would be made by switching the traffic to GSR road services were linked to the need for investment in the railway itself. The line had no chance of survival in the face of this pincer attack. Closure proposals were first issued in 1934 and just as at its inception, when a delegation of local interests had a meeting with a politician, now a deputation went to Dublin to see the minister, Seán Lemass. At least Balfour had the good grace to come to them. Lemass claimed that it would cost at least £40,000 to bring the line up to what he called in an interesting phrase, insurable condition, the implication being that it was already unsafe. In the end it was the state of the roads that gave the line a short stay of execution. Passenger trains were replaced by buses from 1 January 1935 but were reinstated in April of that year as work on the road improvements was still far from complete. The line lasted long enough for that last melancholy special train to run on 17 September 1937 which brought home the remains of the young men killed in the fire at Kirkintilloch, fulfilling for some that ancient prophesy with its passage. On 30 September, hauled appropriately by an Achill bogie, the last train left for Westport, bringing the line's short life to an end.

For a line that closed as long ago as 1937, there are many reminders of the Achill branch which can be explored today. A short stretch of the line, about half a mile in length, remained in use as a siding at Westport station until the 1980s when it was finally lifted. Westport is still of course served by IÉ trains from Dublin and on the first section of the branch from there to Newport much of the trackbed can still be traced and several bridges still survive on this part of the line. The Achill line had only three stations along its 27 miles and there are significant remains at all three places. At Newport a large retaining wall is still doing its job holding back the rest of the hill whose lower reaches had to be excavated to clear a level site for the station. The steel inclined overbridge at the Mallaranny end of the station site is still in place and one building has been converted into an oratory. Some of the other buildings are used by Mayo County Council. Newport viaduct is in superb condition and is a prominent feature of this delightful little town. It is now used to carry a footpath over the Black Oak River. From the Westport end of the viaduct there is an unrestricted view through the former station site to the bridge at its far end. After the railway closed, the road from Newport to Mallaranny was diverted at Burrishole over a new bridge built on the piers of the former railway bridge. These railway relics are still in situ and performing a vital function if unseen by those using the roadway which they are supporting.

At Mallaranny, the former goods shed had been converted into a community hall and the platform used by Achill-bound trains can be made out though the whole site is very overgrown. The water tank, complete with a gauge showing how full it was, stands proudly on its tall brick plinth, though it has not been used to replenish the tank of a locomotive for more than 70 years. It is salutary to reflect that this structure has now been out of use for nearly twice the length of time it was used for the purpose for which it was built. The main station building at Mallaranny is still standing, just. It was badly damaged in a fire, and warning signs urge trespassers or railway archaeologists to keep well clear of it. The only vestiges of its roof are a few charred rafters and sadly one cannot help wondering how long it will be allowed to survive in this extremely dilapidated and dangerous condition.

After viewing the depressing remains of the station at Mallaranny which may not be long for this world, it is refreshing to report that so much of the railway infrastructure remains at Achill that you could almost relay the tracks and start shunting! The site on the shores of Achill Sound which was chosen for the terminus was a large one—in truth probably much too grand for the traffic it had to deal with. Today the main station building is in good condition and advertises itself as a railway hostel. The platform is also intact. The water tank on its plinth is still there at the Mallaranny end of the site. The substantial goods shed stands on its own platform opposite the main station building, and even though it has a good roof it is a bit dilapidated, with broken windows, and is in need of a bit of care. Still it is possible to stand where the buffer stops once were and look along the platform to the station building and with a bit of imagination picture an Achill bogie or a Midland tank at the head of its train of six wheeled coaches and vans and maybe that through coach from the Broadstone full of enthusiastic Edwardian tourists ready for their adventures on Achill.

Chapter 8

A MAGNIFICENT FOLLY:
THE LETTERKENNY &
BURTONPORT EXTENSION
RAILWAY

The Letterkenny & Burtonport Extension Railway first came into my life in singular circumstances. As a student at Queen's in Belfast in the early 1970s, I was one of the two men and a dog who constituted the membership of the now probably long defunct Queen's University Railway Society. A film show was advertised for one particular evening and I ambled down to the Students Union to see what was on offer. The film was on the Burtonport line and it began in black and white with views from the train as it left Letterkenny, the spire of St Eunan's cathedral seen in the distance through the carriage window. The next section featured footage of Churchill and Kilmacrenan stations. This in itself was rare enough but then suddenly—and I still recall my amazement to this day even though I have viewed the footage many times since—it burst into colour. This unique record, probably the first ever colour film of an Irish railway, was made in 1939 when the days of the L&BER were already numbered.

Previous to seeing that remarkable amateur film, even to come across a few black and white photos of the line was rare enough, but here was a series of views from the train showing the rocky grandeur of Barnes Gap and the fragile-looking Owencarrow viaduct. As the train crossed the viaduct, the camera pointed knowingly downwards at the rocky embankment at the north end of the structure, the spot where an Atlantic gale howling down the valley blew a train from Derry off the track in January 1925, causing the death of four passengers. There were shots of a Bedford lorry which was pursuing the train, its final victory in sight though it would yet be postponed for a few years. The condition of the dusty road upon which it was travelling was far from impressive. The highlights of the film for me were the close-ups of one of the line's pair of legendary 4-8-0 tender engines No 10. Its partner No 11 had already been withdrawn in 1933, worn out by years of hard work on the punishing Burtonport line. Built in Leeds by Hudswell Clarke & Co in 1910, these were the only tender engines ever used on an Irish 3 ft gauge line and the only engines of that wheel arrangement to run anywhere in these islands. They would not have looked out of place on the lengthy networks of narrow gauge lines which the British Empire endowed to southern Africa, Australia and parts of India. The tender engines were machines of such size and grandeur that they were in a different league from almost anything else that ever ran on the Irish narrow gauge, with one exception. That exception was also in the Swilly locomotive fleet, the pair of 4-8-4 tank engines which Hudswell Clarke built for the company in 1912.

The film was the work of a remarkable man, Father, later Canon, Tom Doherty who at that time was the curate in The Rosses in north-west Donegal. Somehow or other, possibly from connections in the USA, he got hold of some colour cine film and decided to make a record of the line whose closure, which took place the following year, had been on the cards since the early 1930s. He created an unlikely but impressive epitaph to a railway which was the great epic of the Irish narrow gauge, a magnificent folly almost fated to failure from the day it opened, a line which would never have been built without a vast amount of direct government funding. The politics of this are discussed at some length in Chapter 7. The Burtonport line was built as part of a series of attempts to improve the economy of the congested districts, the official euphemism for that great belt of poverty and deprivation that stretched through most of the west of Ireland from Donegal to Kerry, areas which had never recovered from the disaster of the Great Famine. However well intentioned, whether the L&BER made much difference to the prosperity of the districts it served is open to debate, but from the perspective of those interested in railways it has a resonance which has outlived its final demise over sixty years ago and its physical presence still lingers on in the many relics of the line which survive to this day across the long stretch of County Donegal which it once served.

The early history of the Londonderry & Lough Swilly Railway provided no clues as to what it would be involved with at the end of the nineteenth century. Indeed, it took quite a while for the company to get into its stride. It was first promoted in 1853 to build a broad gauge line from Derry to a pier at Farland Point on the shores of Lough Swilly from where steamers were to run to serve the isolated communities on the shores of this sea lough from which the company took its name. Construction did not begin until 1860. While the work was getting underway, the company got parliamentary approval to build another line branching off its original route at a place that became known as Tooban Junction, west of Burnfoot. This line ran north up the Inishowen Peninsula to the town of Buncrana. The building of the line was one of the last Irish commissions of that great engineer Sir Robert MacNeill who learned his trade as an assistant to Thomas Telford working on the Holyhead Road in the 1830s. Later he was the engineer responsible for building the railway from Dublin to Portadown and to this day the magnificent Craigmore viaduct near Newry, and the sublime little bridge taking the railway over the Newry to Bessbrook road in the style of a classical Egyptian temple, remain monuments to his genius. His other legacy was in the development of his profession in his native land. He was appointed the first professor of civil engineering at Trinity College in Dublin in 1842, a post he held for ten years.

The first section of the L&LSR, the line from Derry to the pier at Farland Point, opened on 31 December 1863 with a service of only two trains in each direction per day. Meanwhile work continued on the Buncrana line which opened in September 1864. The company was virtually broke at this stage and the English firm of Fossick & Hackworth which supplied its first two locomotives had to resort to legal action to obtain payment. The Farland Point branch as it became when the Buncrana line opened was a grave disappointment. The railway company did not own the steamers which served the pier and traffic did not develop in the way anticipated. The line was closed in June 1866 less than three years after it opened, making it one of the shortest lived railways in Ireland, though the tracks were not removed until 1877. The pier itself was dismantled and reassembled at Fahan, where it was linked by a short branch to the Buncrana line. However, this inauspicious start for the L&LSR was more than matched by the second company whose line was to become part of its system.

Proposals to build a railway to Letterkenny had been mooted since around 1850. Two schemes were discussed at various times. One was for a branch from the town to a junction with the Londonderry & Enniskillen line near St Johnstown. The other was for a more circuitous route north along the shores of Lough Swilly which would then head west towards Derry. The first route was authorised by the Letterkenny Railway Company's Act of 1860, though no construction work took place in its wake. Then in 1863 a second Act was obtained, completely changing the route to the second option which would reach Derry over the L&LSR's existing line. This time construction did begin though only about half the company's authorised capital of £100,000 was taken up by investors. Yet another Act of 1866 allowed the company to raise more capital but in the same year the collapse of the London bankers Overend & Guerney sent shock waves through the whole financial system and caused an economic crisis. The additional funds needed to complete the line were not forthcoming, construction work stopped and the half completed line was abandoned.

Two more Acts followed, in 1871 and 1876, attempting to raise the money needed to complete the line. Following the 1876 Act, a Derry-based firm of contractors came up with the idea of building the line to a gauge of 3 ft to save money. This was seized on by the impoverished and increasingly desperate company and yet another bill, this time for a narrow gauge line, was brought forward in 1879. It failed to get through parliament but a second attempt in 1880 was successful. This Act also authorised the L&LSR to convert its existing line to the 3 ft gauge. It had taken six visits to parliament over a 20-year period to get this far. June 1883 finally saw the opening of a railway to Letterkenny. Narrow gauge trains ran over the trackbed of part of the old Farland Point line for the last two miles to a junction with what was still the Swilly's broad gauge line at Tooban. The L&LSR worked the new line from the outset but it would not be until March 1885 that its own line from Derry to Buncrana was converted to the narrow gauge. There was now a compact 3 ft gauge network of around 31 route miles linking the city of Derry to two of the most important towns in its hinterland.

The opening of its railway was far from the end of the troubles of the Letterkenny company. The line had been built with the assistance of a government loan of £50,000. Traffic on the route was poor and not enough revenue was left after the Swilly had been paid to work the line to cover the interest on this debt. In 1887 the Board of Works effectively took over the line. It had taken the LR 23 years to see its objectives finally achieved and yet, only four years after the line at last opened, it lost control of its railway. The new owners entered into an agreement with the L&LSR to work the line for a period of 30 years and thus began what was to be a long and often turbulent relationship between that company and officialdom which would in time see the system greatly expanded but also led to years of wrangling and disputes. It must have been particularly galling for those unwise enough to have invested in the Letterkenny Railway in the course of its chequered financial history to observe what happened next.

At the very time that officialdom in the form of the Board of Works was calling in the LR's mortgages and taking over the company, the Allport Commission was sitting and taking evidence. Out of its report came the Light Railways (Ireland) Act of 1889 which empowered the government to make direct grants to allow light railways to be built in areas of economic deprivation. A total of twelve light railways resulted from the passing of the 1889 Act including two in County Donegal, the Donegal Railway's lines from Stranorlar to Glenties and from Donegal Town to Killybegs. For a number of years there had been various proposals to build railways which were in effect extensions to the Swilly's network. These included a tramway to the north and west of Letterkenny and a line from Buncrana to Carndonagh. The L&LSR was too impoverished to lend any tangible support to these schemes, and although funding for the Carndonagh line was sought under the terms of the 1889 Act, the scheme did not obtain government approval and thus was not built.

It took another Act, the Railways (Ireland) Act of 1896, to provide the finance for the two extensions of the L&LSR system which were built. These were the only lines financed by this piece of legislation, the last fling of railway building as a tool of constructive unionism. The first was relatively straightforward. This was a revival of the plan to extend the existing line to Buncrana some 18 miles north to Carndonagh. On its way up the Inishowen Peninsula this line, which opened in July 1901, provided Ireland with its most northerly station at Ballyliffen, before it turned east to reach Carndonagh. The Carndonagh extension, which was worked throughout its existence by the L&LSR, cost the British taxpayer £98,527 to build. This was virtually small change compared to the cost of the other line, the Letterkenny & Burtonport Extension Railway. There were several candidates on the coast of north-west Donegal which on the face of it had a better claim to being the terminus of a railway from Derry, than Burtonport. It was a place of little consequence and a tiny population. However, it did have a pier and a small fishing fleet and one of the means most favoured for driving economic regeneration in the congested districts was the development of the fishing industry. A railway connection would mean that fish landed at Burtonport could be quickly shipped to market while still fresh. The initial cost of fresh Burtonport fish to the taxpayer was to be in the region of £300,000.

If you draw a straight line on a map and measure it, the distance between Letterkenny and Burtonport is less than 30 miles. However, it was impossible for a railway to take this easy option as in the way was a formidable barrier of mountains. These were broken by valleys which perversely went in the wrong direction for the railway, taking it further out of its way. The result was a line which was a shade under 50 miles long. The many vicissitudes that dogged the line followed from the dysfunctional relationship between government in the shape of the Board of Works which was paying for the building of the line and the Lough Swilly company which had to operate it. The overture to this symphony of squabbling was heard as the Carndonagh line was being built. The Board's engineer insisted on a catalogue of minor and fairly pointless economies which ranged from shortening some of the planned sidings to removing door knockers from station buildings. This was to rise to a cacophony of complaints once the Burtonport line was operating. But before that it had to be built and it was later claimed that many of the problems associated with the line stemmed from its shoddy construction.

The contract to build both extensions was awarded to a London firm, Pauling & Co Ltd. There seem to have been no major issues associated with the building of the Carndonagh line, so perhaps it was the rugged nature of the terrain which lay at the heart of the problems with the Burtonport extension. The course of the line alternated between sections of deep and unstable bog land and rocky outcrops through which a gap had to be blasted. There are stories of sections of newly laid track disappearing into bogs. You can get some sense of the difficulties which nature put in the way of the railway builders even today if you walk on surviving sections of the trackbed. Maintenance of the drainage would have been a major concern for the men who looked after the track in its heyday and of course this has not been attended to now for over 60 years. Nature has taken over and returned the trackbed to the bog from which it had originally been wrested. On the approach to Barnes Gap where the railway and the road shared a narrow defile, the trackbed at one point sits on a ledge high above the road. On one side of the trackbed is the solid rock which had to be blasted away to make room for the rails, yet these were laid mainly on a strip of unstable and sodden bog. The two dilemmas which confronted the railway builders can still be experienced there today within a couple of yards of each other.

Apart from the difficulties associated with the landscape through which it was built, the other baffling thing about the Burtonport line was the manner in which its builders seemed to go out of their way to avoid any habitations that might have provided some traffic for its trains. In this part of north-west Donegal, people have always lived close to the coast. As the terrain meant that a circuitous route had to be followed anyway, one might have thought that a few more miles would not have made much of a difference if this had brought the railway closer to some of the villages it was supposed to be rescuing from economic perdition. Even today, with this part of Donegal a lot more prosperous than it was when the railway was being built, when many of the villages in the area have expanded and straggled out lazily, with new houses built in all directions, some of the stations, Cashelnagore being a prime example, are still miles away from any form of habitation. There are many vistas to be found which take in part of the trackbed with perhaps bridges still intact which are as bereft of houses today as they were when the railway builders were at work.

There was often an arrogance or indifference on the part of nineteenth-century railway builders in relation to where they built their tracks, an assumption that in the absence of any real alternative to their trains, the traffic would always come to them anyway. This was to be the nemesis of many lines once the internal combustion engine spluttered into life in the years following the Great War. In the case of the line to Burtonport, a clue to its eventual downfall is to be found in some of the station names themselves, Dunfanaghy Road, Kincasslagh Road and Dungloe Road, all miles from the villages whose names they bore.

With the opening of the line to Burtonport the L&LSR was now operating a total of 99 miles of 3 ft gauge track. Of these, it owned only the 12½ miles from Derry to Buncrana. The rest of the system had been built and equipped with over half a million pounds of public money. The Swilly company itself was only capitalised to the value of just over £50,000. By contrast with the impoverishment of its early years, it was now paying annual dividends of 7 per cent to its lucky shareholders. Services on the Burtonport line began in March 1903 with only two trains each day on weekdays and one on Sundays, though this was soon increased to three on weekdays at the insistence of the Board of Works. The line is often referred to as the Letterkenny & Burtonport Extension Railway but this term was to some extent a fiction. No such company was ever registered. The railway was owned by the government through the Board of Works but operated by the L&LSR. When first the Carndonagh line and now the L&BER were opened, the Board of Works provided funds to pay for locomotives and rolling stock to run the services. The theory was that the publicly funded stock for the Carndonagh line should only be used on that part of the system. This might have seemed logical to a civil servant but it was treated as nonsense by those operating the railway who largely ignored these strictures. At the start of the last century the Swilly company was chronically short of locomotives and inevitably the management used the nice new engines provided by the Board as they thought fit. This led to many rows with the Board of Works when some eagle-eyed official saw one of the Carndonagh engines merrily puffing along the Letterkenny line. Perhaps to make this type of civil service train-spotting easier, the stock supplied for the Burtonport line was all prominently lettered, L&BER.

The dysfunction between the owners of the line and its operator became markedly apparent at the outset with the Board's choice of locomotives for the new line. They ordered a quartet of 4-6-0 tank engines from Andrew Barclay & Sons of Kilmarnock. These were by all accounts excellent machines but they were far too small to work a line the length of the L&BER. They had small coal bunkers which often had to be replenished en route and their tanks held only 750 gallons of water which meant that trains were often delayed as the locomotives had longer than planned station stops to take more water on board. There were complaints from the Swilly that the Board had not provided enough carriages for the Burtonport line, and the Board of Works in turn complained that its L&BER wagons were being used by the Swilly to carry its own traffic on other parts of the system. The Board of Works was driven by a desire to do things on the cheap wherever possible and the result was a stream of complaints about the service on the Burtonport line. Whether the construction of the line had been motivated by cynical political considerations or noble aspirations to bring a measure of prosperity to the congested districts of north-west Donegal by providing the area with a decent link to the rest of the country, the reality on the ground in the years after the line opened was that of a poor service operated with inadequate resources which was to the benefit of nobody.

The paint on the line's stations was hardly dry when the complaints started. In June 1903 Edward McFadden, the MP for Donegal East, questioned George Wyndham, the Chief Secretary for Ireland, about recent events on the line. 'I beg to ask the Chief Secretary to the Lord Lieutenant of Ireland whether he is aware that the Lough Swilly Railway Company which works the new

Letterkenny to Burtonport Extension Railway, County Donegal, failed to provide sufficient accommodation for passengers on the line on the occasion of the hiring fair at Letterkenny on 15th May last and whether, in view of the overcrowding of compartments on that occasion, and of the fact that a number of passengers on the same occasion were put into goods wagons and cattle trucks and charged the same fares as persons in third class passenger carriages, and that the morning train to Letterkenny from Burtonport was an hour late in arriving, and the evening train was an hour-and-a-half late in leaving Letterkenny, and that a number of persons were unable to obtain travelling accommodation in the train at Letterkenny Station and at Old Town Station, the Board of Works, with whom the Lough Swilly Company entered into agreement for working the line, will see that the terms of the agreement are carried out and sufficient accommodation is provided for the travelling public.'

The Chief Secretary's response to these complaints was predictably bland and non-committal, expressing the hope that matters would improve when the line had been in operation for a longer period. That proved to be far from the case. A lot of the problems with the Burtonport line seem to have stemmed from the regular failures of locomotives. The Swilly's works, if they could be dignified with that term, at Pennyburn in Derry were poorly equipped to maintain the line's locomotives. The lack of an engine shed at Letterkenny meant that if anything went wrong with an engine out on the extension, assistance could be a long time coming. The constant complaints led to the Board of Works asking the distinguished former manager of the Belfast & County Down and Midland Great Western Railways, Joseph Tatlow, to conduct an enquiry into the working of the line. While this was going on, the L&LSR took matters into its own hands and ordered the two 4-8-0s from Hudswell Clarke in Leeds. At last proper motive power for the line was available. There was no need to stop for coal as the big tender engines could carry enough for a round trip from Derry to Burtonport and yet, because their weight was spread over six axles, they actually caused less wear and tear to the track than some of the tank engines which had hitherto been used.

The early 1900s were years in which all the Irish railway companies came under critical scrutiny from their customers and local politicians. They were widely perceived as being inefficient and charging much higher rates than were applicable in other parts of the kingdom. Many wanted to see the private companies abolished and the whole national network taken into public ownership. In 1906 to calm things down the government did what governments often do when they want to calm things down, they appointed a commission of enquiry. The Vice-Regal Commission on Irish Railways sat and took evidence from 1906 to 1909, but when its findings were published in 1910 two reports were presented. The minority report supported the status quo whilst the majority report favoured the creation of an Irish Railways Authority to take control of the whole network. Once again the government did what governments do best, which was nothing, and the fascinating might-have-been which the majority report suggested, that of a united national network under one management, never came about. Had it happened, who knows, this book might have had a much shorter list of abandoned railways to draw on.

The continuing rows swirling around the Burtonport line inevitably were brought up in evidence before the Vice-Regal Commission. Even though it had not been intended that it should get involved in disputes like this, its chairman Sir Charles Scotter, who was also the chairman of the English London & South Western Railway, offered to act as a mediator between the warring parties, the Board of Works and the Swilly company. The terms of the Scotter award as the settlement was called are a testimony to some of the problems which had bedevilled the line to date. Its provisions largely vindicated the L&LSR and pointed the finger towards the parsimony of the Board who for a start had to agree to pay the Swilly money which was still outstanding from the construction phase. An engine shed was at last to be built at Letterkenny at a cost of £2,000 to the Board, and an additional passing place was to be provided at Kilmacrenan station. The biggest single element in the award was a payment of £7,000 by the Board for additional rolling stock to work the line. This was spent on two new 4-6-2 tank engines, an extra carriage and nearly 30 new wagons.

Following the Scotter award peace or rather a sort of truce broke out in the hills of north-west Donegal for a few years. The Swilly continued its flirtation with big engines when it ordered its two 4-8-4 tanks in 1912 from Hudswell Clarke and at last the company had available a small fleet of engines which could cope with the lengthy Burtonport line. However, the criticisms of how the line was being operated soon began to rise again in volume. In 1917 the Board of Works decided to swing into action. Using a clause of the Railways (Ireland) Act of 1896 which permitted it to appoint an independent figure to inspect and report on the operation of a line built with public money under the terms of the Act, Joseph Tatlow was again invited to Donegal to inspect the L&BER.

If the Scotter award had been a vindication for the Swilly company, Tatlow's report presented a devastating picture of a line which was badly run and badly maintained. He started with stark criticism of the state of the company's Graving Dock terminus in Derry where he found that cattle were frequently unloaded at the passenger platform, leading to his description of the place as *malodorous*. Tatlow criticised the state of the engines and, in turn, punctuality on the line. In January 1917 two trains were over four hours late, and out of 432 trains run thus far in that year, only seven arrived at their destination on time. There were faults with some of the signalling equipment on the extension. In extremis, this could have led to the danger of two trains being allowed on to the one section of single track at the same time, with potentially horrendous results. Lack of station staff led to men who should have been employed on maintaining the track being diverted to other duties and many carriages ran without lighting of any kind.

The conclusion to Tatlow's report included the following observations: 'The Burtonport line is not in good condition and has not been efficiently worked, maintained or developed. Everything has for years past been allowed to run down; the direction and management has been characterised by extreme parsimony; the disabled condition of the engines is undoubtedly due to want of proper upkeep which must have been going on for years. The state of the permanent way shows a want of proper maintenance and the condition of the stations, buildings and of the carriages, all speak of neglect.' This was game set and match to the Board of Works and the immediate result of Tatlow's findings was the resignation of the Chairman of the L&LSR, Sir John Mc Farland, who had been on the board of the company since 1884. The generous dividends which the Swilly shareholders had been enjoying for years had come at the price of letting the whole undertaking become ramshackle and rundown. Under the terms of the 1896 Act, the Privy Council now decided to appoint a manager to take over the running of the line. Strangely the person elevated to this position was the Swilly's own General Manager, Henry Hunt, who had joined the company from the English Great Central Railway in 1916. He seems to have impressed Tatlow during his tour of inspection and he had probably not been in the job long enough to have been tainted by the culture of neglect and penny pinching which seems to have been how the L&LSR managed the L&BER. Perhaps the company had learned this method of running the railway from the example set by the Board of Works when the line was being constructed years before.

Scarcely had the ramifications of the Tatlow report been absorbed before another and even more challenging set of circumstances began to unfold. The war against the British presence in Ireland was conducted with some vigour on Swilly territory. There were several British naval and military bases in and around Derry on the shores of Lough Foyle and Lough Swilly and their personnel provided targets for the insurgents. During the Great War the railway had carried a lot of extra traffic emanating from these facilities, but now there was a concerted effort of both attacks on trains and intimidation of railway staff to impede all military traffic. Many staff were suspended or dismissed for refusing to work such trains. The remote area served by the L&BER was ideal territory for guerilla attacks and many stations were held up or had their goods stores looted. Several trains were derailed when they ran into boulders which had been deliberately placed on the line. There was no shortage of this type of ammunition out on the extension. Such was the disruption and the frequency of the attacks that the Burtonport line eventually had to be closed for three months at the end of 1920.

The treaty which created the Irish Free State instigated the next phase of violence as the new state attempted to assert its authority over those opposed to the settlement. The Troubles seemed to have lingered on for longer in this part of Donegal than in the rest of the Free State. The last attack on a railway in the whole country took place as late as September 1925 when a train from Derry to Burtonport was derailed between Crolly and Kincasslagh Road when it ran into the weapon of choice in these parts, boulders which had been placed on the line. However bad and disruptive had been the immediate effects of the Troubles, it was the long-term economic consequences of the political settlement that followed in their wake which really was to cause terminal damage to the whole Lough Swilly system. Customs posts were erected in 1923 along the new border. If there was any logic to county boundaries, the city of Derry or at least the greater part of it on the west bank of the Foyle should really have been in County Donegal. But it was not, it was in the new state of Northern Ireland as were the three or four miles of Swilly track which led from the city to the border. This meant that as the line entered Northern Ireland it did not become part of the GSR in 1925. However, it also meant that Derry was now cut off from its natural economic hinterland in County Donegal both by a line on a map and by different tariff regimes on either side of that line.

The days of the 7 per cent dividends rapidly became a distant memory as the finances of the L&LSR deteriorated, probably more quickly than those of any other Irish railway at the time. There were no dividends at all after 1923. The only positives in those years were the ending of wartime government control which had been imposed on all the Irish companies in 1917 and the return to the fold of the L&BER. Hunt ceased to be its government-appointed custodian in June 1922 and reverted to being the General Manager of the whole system. Since the Privy Council's intervention, he had been in the very odd position of being their manager of the L&BER while continuing to be the company's manager of the rest of their lines.

Adding to its woes, a Swilly train was to be involved in a tragic and dramatic accident on the Owencarrow viaduct in the winter of 1925. There had been earlier derailments caused by gale force winds raging in off the Atlantic across the bleak and treeless uplands. Shortly after the L&BER opened in February 1906, two carriages were derailed by wind when crossing the viaduct, though fortunately they remained on the structure. A train was derailed by gales near Dunfanaghy Road on Christmas Day in 1922 and again in 1923 between Crolly and Kincasslagh Road. The evening of 30 January 1925 was marked by strong winds coming in from the Atlantic. The 5.15pm train from Derry left Kilmacrenan shortly before 8.00pm to begin the undulating climb through Barnes Gap before dropping down into the valley which was crossed by the Owencarrow viaduct. It should have reached Creeslough, the next station, in about 25 minutes. Trains were subject to a speed restriction of 10 mph as they rounded the sharp curve which led on to the viaduct. It was an odd-looking structure, 380 yards long but not more than about 30 ft high, and consisted of a mixture of girder spans with a stone embankment followed by two masonry arches at its north end. Trains heading for Burtonport were on a falling gradient until they reached that stone embankment at the north end of the viaduct when the gradient abruptly changed to 1 in 50 as the line climbed out of the valley through which ran the Owencarrow River. The line ran due south to north across the viaduct and it was thus exposed to the full force of the severe westerly gale which was blowing down the valley that night. The train was almost across the viaduct when, as it was passing over the stone embankment, a gust of wind picked up a six wheeled carriage and flipped it on to its roof, landing it partly on the rocky embankment and partly on the parapet of the first of the masonry arches. Other vehicles were derailed but all the dead were in that six wheeler. Three died at the scene, and a fourth passenger succumbed later in hospital in Letterkenny. After the accident the company added ballast in the form of heavy slabs of iron to all carriages used on the Burtonport line.

Despite the company receiving some £68,000 in compensation from the British government for the period when they had been in control of the railway from 1917 onwards, the Swilly's finances were in a bad way as early as 1924. Even though the roads in north Donegal were very poor, unregulated competition from privately owned lorries began to hit the company's revenues. From 1924 onwards the company needed grants from both governments to keep its services running. The deposed former chairman, Sir John McFarland, was quoted in the *Railway Magazine* of April 1925, speaking at the company's annual general meeting, '. . . the financial position of the company is desperate and unless something is done in regard to the high wages paid to employees, the company will have to close down.' He had learned nothing. Wages had risen during the war throughout the whole economy but his solution, a reversion to the obsessive drive for savings which had reduced the L&BER to a state of perilous disrepair in the previous decade, was not going to turn back the tide. The subsidies from the two governments were to continue into the 1930s when a radically different approach to dealing with its problems was devised.

By 1930 the company was close to insolvency. Henry Hunt left the L&LSR in 1931 and was replaced by James Whyte, a local man who had been with the company for many years and was an accountant rather than the railwayman that Hunt had been. In time Whyte turned the fortunes of the L&LSR around but in doing so he transformed it from being the operator of the second largest narrow gauge system in Ireland into a bus company. The first line to go was the extension from Buncrana to Carndonagh which closed completely in December 1935, a mere 34 years after it had opened, hardly a vindication that the near £100,000 of public money which it had cost to build was money well spent. Also in the early 1930s, the company began to buy out scores of private bus and lorry operators and started to expand its own road services. Dividends began to be paid again to shareholders as the company moved its services from road to rail. As early as 1931 an attempt to replace at least some of the passenger services on the Burtonport line with buses fell foul of Donegal County Council who claimed the buses were damaging its fragile roads. One might have thought the reverse was also true and wonder at what state the buses would be in after a few months in service on the Council's roads. The buses were withdrawn and the line was patched up with second-hand materials salvaged from the closure of the Carndonagh route. In 1935 passenger trains to Buncrana were replaced by buses apart from on Thursdays and Saturdays during the summer. By now it was clear to all who cared to notice that the days of the remaining Swilly rail services were numbered. Thank goodness, among those who took notice was Father Doherty who made his remarkable film in the summer of 1939.

The start of World War Two did not immediately affect the planned run down of rail services. The withdrawal of all services on the L&BER and passenger trains between Derry and Letterkenny took place in June 1940 and demolition of the line began from Burtonport in August of that year. This led to a wave of protests and direct action in blocking the activities of those dismantling the railway. Some claimed that as the Swilly had not built the line in the first place, they had no right to rip it up now.

The matter passed to Dublin where the Department of Industry and Commerce decreed in November 1940 that the lifting of the line could go ahead. However, by now the reality of the severe wartime shortages of oil had become apparent and the line was given a temporary reprieve. Goods services were reinstated as far as Gweedore in February and later passengers were conveyed in a carriage on the daily goods on the line.

The engines used on these wartime trains were fuelled mainly on turf, owing to the chronic coal shortage which bedevilled all railway services in the Free State at that time. Little maintenance was done to the worn-out track and by June 1947 the stay of execution was over, with the last goods train running from Letterkenny to Gweedore, thus finally ending the chequered career of the Letterkenny & Burtonport Extension Railway. The rest of the Swilly was not far behind it, with the last goods trains running to Letterkenny in June 1953 and to Buncrana in August of that year.

Though it was open for only 44 years, few railways in Ireland had such a turbulent history as the Burtonport line. It would never have been built without the huge sums of government money poured into it and that begs the question as to whether this was money wisely spent. In more recent times the EU has lavished large amounts of money to improve the infrastructure of the Irish Republic, mostly in the form of road building projects. Such investments are not judged by their immediate impact which is often only noticeable at a local level in so far as they enable people to get from A to B a bit more quickly. Their greater significance is in their contribution to the economic development of the country. It is on this basis that we must attempt to judge the contribution which the L&BER made to bringing prosperity to the impoverished parts of north-west Donegal which it served and in truth it is hard to see that it made any real impact. It did not stop the decline in the area's population or stimulate the development of any new industries. There were fishing boats at Burtonport before the line was built and they are still there today, but it never became the hub of a major fishery.

The aspirations of the politicians who were enthusiastic about such projects were debased in this instance by the grudging and parsimonious way in which their civil servants at the Board of Works oversaw the building of the line. Undoubtedly parts of it were constructed in a shoddy way but then it had to traverse some of the worst imaginable terrain in Ireland. If it was shaped in this deleterious way by its geography, it was the landscape which also gave the line its enduring appeal. The thought of the Swilly's big eight coupled engines forging through this inhospitable landscape on track which in places was virtually floating on top of the bog and was almost imperceptibly rising and falling under their wheels, as they battled severe gradients and gales howling in from the Atlantic, is enough to send a frisson of pleasure down the spines of all railway romantics. We will pass on the less attractive realities of travel on the L&BER, a journey from Derry to Burtonport which would have taken the best part of five hours at an average speed including station stops of between 15 and 20 mph, sitting on a wooden slatted seat in a carriage which had no proper heating and, if the journey was on an evening train, probably in the dark.

Nothing remains of the Swilly passenger station in Letterkenny today. But the adjacent terminus of the other narrow gauge line which once served the town, the County Donegal Railways branch from Strabane, is still standing and even plays its part in public transport in its role as a Bus Éireann office. The wild and barren wilderness through which the extension ran is still there to entice us today as are many remains of the line itself. The peaks of Muckish and Errigal brood over the country and would have been visible to passengers on the line for many miles. Nothing encapsulates the folly and the grandeur of the line more than the section through Barnes Gap. The abandoned trackbed is perched on a ledge above the road, the formation blasted out of the solid rock. The piers which supported the girder bridge over the road there still stand, as elegant as the ruins of an ancient temple. Beyond this, the line ran downhill and then curved sharply to cross the valley of the Owencarrow River on its famous viaduct. There is no example of railway archaeology in Ireland as impressive as the remains of the viaduct itself. The stone piers which carried its girders across the valley and the two metal supports on the valley's bottom stand out in the landscape like some latter-day Neolithic monument. Even though the girders have gone, the differing heights of the piers show how the line dipped towards the centre of the structure. The fatal arches on which that carriage was impaled in 1925 at the north end of the viaduct are also still there.

Other artifacts abound along the course of the line. The house built for the crossing keeper at No 9 Gates, the first set after the viaduct, is occupied and is probably in much better condition today than it was under its original parsimonious owners. Cashelnagore station is still there in splendid and authentic isolation and there are sections of trackbed and bridges to be found most of the way to Burtonport where the site of the station and part of the trackbed are easily identifiable. The line has long gone but its memory and its presence lingers on and tracing its relics adds another pleasure to a journey through this wild but magnificent part of County Donegal.

Chapter 9

RAILS TO VALENTIA HARBOUR

Samuel Johnson, the great eighteenth-century lexicographer, is reputed to have referred to one of Ireland's most visited tourist attractions, then as now, the Giant's Causeway, as, 'worth seeing? Yes; but not worth going to see'. What he would have made of the Ring of Kerry is not recorded for he never got that far but today there is no disputing that this scenic route starting from Killarney and running around the coast of the Iveragh Peninsula is one of the country's great tourist hot spots. The final stretch of our journey along some of the railway lines throughout Ireland from which the trains have long departed takes us down the western side of that peninsula to explore another of the Balfour lines and one which had a strong claim to have been the most scenic railway line in the whole of the island. This was the branch of the Great Southern & Western Railway that ran from a junction at Farranfore, on the Mallow to Tralee line, to Valentia Harbour.

This part of County Kerry is one where the natural beauty is on a monumental scale. It includes Ireland's highest peak, Carrantuohill, which rises to 3,406 ft. This was a name I first became aware of in another context at Omagh station one day many years ago. I remember spelling it out from the brass nameplate on the blue driving wheel splasher of the Great Northern's S class 4-4-0 No 173. It was much later when I discovered this mysterious name was that of a mountain, as were those of her sisters. While the Iveragh Peninsula holds evidence of human settlement dating back to the Iron Age, its recent history is the familiar one of a decline in population of perhaps two-thirds in the century following the Great Famine. While the people who lived on Valentia Island at the bottom of the peninsula suffered less badly than those on the mainland during the Famine because of the richness of the fisheries that surrounded them on all sides, this whole area of south Kerry was defined as one of the congested districts in the 1890s.

Valentia had figured in the dreams of railway promoters long before Arthur Balfour and the Light Railways (Ireland) Act, which eventually enabled the railway to Valentia to be constructed, were ever heard of. Throughout the nineteenth century various hugely ambitious schemes were mooted to build railways linking some of the great natural harbours on the western seaboard of Ireland to the east coast. The government's own Irish Railway Commissioners, who were given the task of planning a national network of railways for Ireland in the 1830s, identified Valentia and Berehaven in County Cork as possible sites for a new port which would be connected by rail to Dublin. The motivation behind these plans was the creation of a harbour where vessels carrying mail from the New World would call. The mail would be whisked across Ireland to the east coast to be taken on the short sea crossing to Wales, and then on by rail to London and other British cities, thus saving the several days it would have taken those ships to reach a port in Britain. The engineer Charles Vignoles, who was involved in the planning of Ireland's first railway, the Dublin & Kingstown, advocated one of these schemes during the Railway Mania of the 1830s, a line from Valentia to Dublin.

Similar grandiose proposals which were mooted throughout the nineteenth century identified such unlikely spots as Kilrush in County Clare and Belmullet in County Mayo as potential sites for this great new trans-Atlantic hub. Almost inevitably none of these schemes ever got off the drawing board. However, Valentia Island was to play a unique role in the development of transatlantic communications but in a very different way to that envisaged by those early railway schemes. In August 1858 the European end of the first transatlantic telegraph cable was landed at Knightstown on the island. It stretched from there across the ocean floor to Newfoundland. The first successful transatlantic message was transmitted on the 16th of that month and was followed by an exchange of celebratory greetings between Queen Victoria and American President James Buchanan to usher in a new era in communications.

The first railway to penetrate the Kingdom of Kerry was the 40 mile line from Mallow to Killarney, opened in 1853 by the Killarney Junction Railway. This company had strong financial backing from the GS&WR. By this time Killarney was already beginning to make its mark as a destination for tourists, and in 1854 the KJR opened the first railway-owned hotel in Ireland, later to be better known as the Great Southern Hotel. Killarney remained a terminus until 1859 when the line was extended the 22 miles to Tralee by the Tralee & Killarney Railway. From the day this extension opened to the present virtually every passenger train from Mallow to Tralee and those travelling in the other direction has had to reverse into or out of Killarney station. Such shunting of loaded passenger trains was a rare practice and one usually frowned on by the Board of Trade, the arbitrators of railway practice in the nineteenth century. One of the stations opened on the line to Tralee was at Farranfore, later to be the junction for the Valentia branch.

Throughout this book, in order to avoid the minefield which surrounds the spelling of many Irish place names, the plan, which has more or less worked up to this point, has always been to use the spellings favoured by the railway companies. However, in the case of the terminus of this branch line that plan has become somewhat derailed. When the line opened, the GS&WR used the spelling Valencia on the station nameboard there and in its timetables. The original GS&WR station nameboard at the terminus photographed in 1934 still displayed that spelling. A few years later, this was replaced by a new Great Southern Railways bilingual board of the type which was introduced across the network at that time and will have been familiar to older readers as many of them survived well into the CIÉ era. The new GSR board continued to use Valencia as its English version and indeed this board remained in place until the line closed. However, by 1950 CIÉ had changed the spelling to Valentia in its timetables and on the maps which accompanied them and as this is the version used in most printed sources in the second half of the last century, even though it never actually was used at the station itself, it is the one I have settled on.

As well as the grand designs mentioned earlier for railways in connection with a new transatlantic port, there were several proposals from the 1850s onwards for local lines connecting Valentia to the Tralee to Mallow route. Like the earlier schemes, no construction work on any of these lines was ever started. Then in 1871 an Act was granted to the Killorglin Railway authorising the construction of a line 12 miles long from Farranfore to Killorglin. As often happened in Ireland when a rural line such as this was mooted, not a lot happened as the capital to build it could not be raised. This is not surprising as the population of Killorglin was no more than about 1,000 at the time and it is hard to believe that the traffic on offer from the line would have provided any sort of acceptable return on the cost of building the railway.

In this instance not a lot happened for a period of over 10 years until 1882 when the GS&WR took over the powers of the independent but hitherto ineffectual Killorglin company and engaged a contractor to build the branch. The catalyst which got construction underway was the assistance provided by baronial guarantees. In this case the Grand Jury of County Kerry approved a guarantee of 5 per cent interest for a term of 35 years on £60,000 of the capital employed to build the line. The new railway, which had intermediate stations at Molahiffe, Castlemaine and

Milltown, opened on 15 January 1885. As was typical of most minor Irish lines, there were ten level crossings scattered along its first ten miles. The only significant engineering feature was the viaduct which took the line over the River Luane near Killorglin on three 105 ft long bowstring girder spans. This viaduct, like the other two impressive engineering works on the branch, Gleensk viaduct and the great girder bridge across the River Fertha at Cahirciveen, is still standing 50 years after the line closed. Unlike the other two it is possible to walk legally along the bridge over the River Luane today.

The government-appointed Allport Commission which reported in 1888 had included among its recommendations the extension of the existing line from Killorglin to Valentia Harbour. The Balfour Act of 1889 provided the financial means to achieve this. The GS&WR was given a grant of £85,000 by the government to build the 27 mile long extension. Unusually construction was undertaken by the railway company itself and not contracted out. Work began in 1890, and given the difficult nature of the terrain through which the line had to be driven and the size and complexity of the two great engineering set pieces required at Gleensk and Cahirciveen, it was completed commendably quickly. Train services from Farranfore through to Valentia Harbour commenced on 12 September 1893. The line was single track throughout, with passing places at Glenbeigh, Mountain Stage and Kells.

This was a line of great contrasts. The first 12 miles from Farranfore to Killorglin were relatively level and it was not until after Glenbeigh, seven miles beyond Killorglin, that the climbing started in earnest. From there to the next station, Mountain Stage three miles further on, the line climbed relentlessly on gradients as steep as 1 in 59. The station at Mountain Stage, where a passing loop was provided, was unusual in that its platforms did not face each other. In railway parlance the platforms were staggered. For the next six miles from Mountain Stage to Kells the course the railway took and the scenery through which it passed can only be described as spectacular. For much of the way it ran parallel to the coast, with views from the train across Dingle Bay. On a clear day it would have been possible to see the smoke from a narrow gauge train on the Tralee & Dingle Railway on the other side of the bay. For part of the journey after Mountain Stage the line ran along a ledge hewn out of the hillside. At one point a mile and a half beyond Mountain Stage the track passed through what was described as a covered way. This was a roof built over the track for 50 yards to deflect rocks falling off the hillside. The side facing the sea was left open. In other parts of Europe such as the Swiss Alps this would have been described as an avalanche shelter.

Two short tunnels brought the line through the slopes of Drung Hill before it turned inland to come to the magnificent Gleensk viaduct which took the line 70 ft above the river in the valley below on eleven curved steel spans. Gleensk viaduct is still today an elegant and awe-inspiring structure. We can only imagine what it would have been like to travel over it as an elderly J15 0-6-0 and her short train of six wheeled coaches screeched round the 10 chain radius curve of the viaduct, her driver conscientiously and wisely adhering to the 10 mph speed restriction which was in place there. Throughout the whole existence of the line because of the severity of the curves here and elsewhere on the branch, most types of the longer and more comfortable bogie coaches were banned from use between Farranfore and Valentia lest their buffers locked on these curves which could have led to a derailment. This allowed the line to remain one of the last places in these islands which regularly saw the use of elderly six wheeled coaches which looked particularly incongruous when hauled by one of CIÉ's new C class diesel locomotives following their arrival in the mid-1950s.

For trains heading to Valentia, the climbing was over after they had reached Kells station, seven miles from Mountain Stage. Here the fireman could at last take a breather as from there it was down hill all the way to the terminus. However, a service heading in the other direction had to face a climb of over four miles on gradients as severe as 1 in 40, which took it from sea level at Cahirciveen to reach Kells station which was 404 ft above sea level. The line swept over the river on its long low girder bridge to reach Cahirciveen station and the only habitation of any size encountered since Killorglin, 24 miles away. As long as the history of Ireland is recounted this modest but attractive Kerry town will have a footnote in it as the boyhood home of Daniel O'Connell. As early as 1825 he had been a director of the ambitious Leinster & Munster Railway, which was almost a national network in itself, combining a Dublin to Belfast line with elements of what later would emerge as the GS&WR. Though the Liberator passed away close to 50 years before the Valentia branch reached Cahirciveen, I am sure he would have approved if it. The town's other claim to fame in the nineteenth century was that it was one of the few places where there was some action during the abortive Fenian Rising of 1867. In February of that year rebels attacked an isolated coastguard station, robbed a gentleman's house and stole his horses, and shot a policeman before moving off in the direction of Killarney. Shortly afterwards in 1869 and probably not unconnected with these events, work began on the construction of a huge new Royal Irish Constabulary barracks close to the river and later the railway. Today this has been restored and converted into a heritage centre.

Beyond Cahirciveen the line more or less petered out as it ran beside the river to reach its terminus at Valentia Harbour two and a half miles further on. Here there was a mean little station made of corrugated iron, a run round loop and a siding close to where the boats which served Valentia Island tied up. Corrugated iron was used for other stations on the extension and was even used to construct the engine shed at Cahirciveen. The latter was the most westerly in both Ireland and Europe and the station at Valentia Harbour had the same claim to fame. This was also as far as it was possible to go from Dublin on the tracks of Ireland's largest railway, the GS&WR. The station at Valentia Harbour was about 235 miles from Kingsbridge.

The purpose of this and the other lines built with government funding at this time was to encourage economic development in the areas they served. One important aspect of the local economy which the Congested Districts Board was always keen to encourage in many of the districts it served was the development of the fishing industry. The Board built piers and improved harbours down the whole of the west coast from Donegal to Cork and Kerry. The new railways had the potential to transport fish quickly to market while it was still fresh and there is some evidence that the Valentia line was a success in this respect. In the 1890s the Board of Trade published statistics on the amount of fish landed at Irish ports and forwarded by rail. This rose throughout the decade from 10,800 tons in 1894 to 17,445 tons in 1899. Of the ports newly connected in that decade by the lines built with government funding, the Valentia branch consistently handled the largest tonnages, rising from 1,175 in 1894 to 2,959 tons in 1899. In that final year of the nineteenth century this contrasted with 861 tons from Clifden and a very modest 281 tons on the Achill line.

The other industry which the railway helped to encourage was, as we have seen elsewhere, tourism and the epicentre of this in Ireland, then as now, was Killarney. Royal patronage helped to enhance Killarney's reputation, with visits by Queen Victoria in 1861 and by one of her many offspring, Prince Arthur, in 1869 and from then on it never looked back. The GS&WR, in addition to that first hotel in Killarney dating from the 1854, opened others in the vicinity at Caragh Lake, Kenmare, Parknasilla and Waterville. These were operated by a subsidiary of the railway company, Southern Hotels, which later merged with its parent early in the last century. In addition to the grand hotels there were even a couple of what might be described today as budget hotels in the group. These were located at Killarney and Parknasilla and were suitable for the less affluent of Victorian and Edwardian tourists. The one at Killarney had, like the Great Southern Hotel, its own private entrance from the station. The hotel at Caragh Lake was on the Valentia line.

In order to promote the many areas it served which had the potential to attract tourists, the GS&WR published at the turn of the nineteenth century several editions of a guidebook called *The Sunny Side of Ireland*. This described the hotel at Caragh Lake as being five minutes walk from the station. Dooks, the next station beyond Caragh Lake, had a nine-hole golf course nearby. Guests staying at the Caragh Lake Hotel had honorary membership of the golf club conferred on them for the duration of their stay and could play on the course. Dooks was what was known as a flag station where a signal had to be given by prospective passengers to the driver if they wanted to board the train. Any intending to alight had to inform the Guard beforehand.

One has to admire both the vigorous promotion of the tourist industry by the GS&WR and the powers of endurance of some of their potential clients. In 1906 the GS&WR and Britain's Great Western Railway opened a new steamer service from Rosslare to Fishguard and railways connecting these ports to the rest of the network on either side of the Irish Sea. In the autumn of that year, the companies advertised a day trip from Bristol to Killarney. Passengers left Bristol's Temple Meads station at 8.51pm and arrived at Fishguard at 1.25am the next morning where they embarked on a steamer for Rosslare. On arrival at the Irish port, a special train took them to Killarney, arriving there just before midday. These day trippers had only about seven hours to explore the delights of Killarney before they had to get back to the station in time to catch their train back to Rosslare at 6.40pm. They eventually arrived back in Bristol some 35 hours after they had set out. Even allowing for the colourful nature of much of the advertising at the time, this was a very liberal interpretation of the concept of a day trip. The fares for this marathon were 12 shillings from Bristol and 10 shillings and six pence for any citizens of Cardiff mad enough to join in the adventure from the Welsh city.

One characteristic is common to most of the minor lines

discussed in these pages. Despite the great expenditure lavished on their construction, the service provided when they eventually opened was sparse to say the least. In this respect the Valentia line was no exception. In 1900 there were just two through trains from Farranfore to Valentia Harbour, though there were three trains in the other direction. Killorglin had the benefit of an extra service from the junction. There was also a short working from there to Cahirciveen which arrived at 8.26am. As the engine shed and the turntable at the southern end of the branch were at Cahirciveen, there was an additional train from there to Valentia, leaving at 8.00am and arriving at the terminus seven minutes later. This was hardly to cater for the commuter traffic at that hour, rather it was to get the engine and carriages to Valentia Harbour to form the 8.25am service to Farranfore. This exercise was repeated in the evening to get the stock which had formed the 4.00pm from Farranfore to Valentia Harbour back to Cahirciveen for servicing. The time allowed for a train to travel the 40 miles to Valentia from the junction was around two hours, and slightly longer in the other direction.

The line lost its passenger services for a short time because of the coal shortages occasioned by the bitter winter of 1947. They were suspended on 24 February, resuming exactly three months later on 24 May. Apart from that, though the ownership of the line had changed twice since 1900, the pattern of services scarcely changed at all in 50 years. The CIÉ summer timetable from 1950 offered the familiar two through trains along the whole length of the line from Farranfore to Valentia Harbour, with an extra service from Killorglin to Cahirciveen. There were still three trains in the other direction. A feature of this line was that one of the trains was usually mixed, conveying both goods wagons and passenger coaches. This practice lingered on many of CIÉ's quieter branch lines into the 1950s.

The board of CIÉ deserves some praise for at least making an attempt to modernise its railways in the 1950s, unlike its counterpart in Northern Ireland whose main aim seemed to be to get rid of them as quickly as possible. In 1955 the first of the 60 Metropolitan Vickers built A class diesel locomotives were introduced to haul main line trains. These were followed in 1956/57 by the 34 members of the less powerful C class locos, from the same makers, intended for use on branch lines and secondary routes. The C class diesels began to be used on the branch lines in County Kerry but they never replaced steam entirely. The redoubtable J15 class 0-6-0s, the most numerous type of steam locomotive used in Ireland, the first of which was built as long ago as 1866, continued to be used on the Valentia line and the nearby Kenmare branch, the other former GS&WR Balfour line in the county, throughout the 1950s. A total of 118 of those locomotives entered service over a period of 37 years, the great majority of them being built at Inchicore works. No other type of GS&WR engine exceeded 20 in number. Several decades later, one of the C class diesels was for some years preserved on a few yards of track close to the viaduct at Cahirciveen. It suffered at the hands of vandals there and has now been removed to a site near another disused viaduct, that which took the line to Mallow over the River Suir in Waterford. While the government's attitude towards the railways in the Republic was less negative than in the north, given the official pursuit of the unattainable in the form of a public transport system which paid its way, it was almost inevitable in the climate of the time that the days of the Valentia branch were numbered. It was yet another victim of Todd Andrews and his board and lost its services from 1 February 1960, though a few cattle specials were operated up until August of that year.

The line from Killorglin to Valentia was probably the most scenic stretch of railway in the whole of Ireland. If by some miracle it had survived it would surely have been a major tourist attraction today, though realistically there was never a chance of this happening. It is doubtful if it ever made a profit throughout its whole existence though, as was the case with all branch lines, it had value in that it fed traffic on to the rest of the network and in its heyday the Valentia line played a significant role in bringing tourists into the area. Apart from the three great engineering features—the bridge over the River Luane, Gleensk viaduct and the bridge across the river at Cahirciveen—there are many other reminders of the line which can be viewed today. The former goods shed at Killorglin is all that remains of this once important station but the platform, station building and signal box at Glenbeigh are still in existence and in good order. It was noted earlier that some of the stations were built with corrugated iron, hardly the most elegant and long-lasting of materials. Despite this, the appearance of the beautifully restored station building at Kells transcends the modest material from which it is constructed. The station building, now used by the local community, is in pristine condition, as is the adjacent signal box. Both platforms there are also extant.

Kells station is the final stop on our journey and it is good to end it on such a positive note. To continue this tone of optimism, it is fair to say that there is a wealth of goodwill towards the railways which remain in operation in Ireland today. I don't think I have ever met anyone who is actively against railways or who felt they should all be ripped up as they had transcended their usefulness. Many families have a railway connection in their histories, and most of us will still stop to look at or wave at a steam-hauled special train as it bowls along. After years of decline Irish railways are on the up once again. In 2010 passenger services resumed on the line between Limerick and Athenry for the first time since 1976. Passenger trains began to operate between Cork and Midleton in 2009 and on 3 September 2010 passenger trains began to run again on part of the former MGWR Navan branch as far as a new park-and-ride station near the M3 motorway at Dunboyne. The last time a scheduled passenger train called at Dunboyne was in January 1947.

It remains to be seen whether the present difficult economic conditions will put a brake on other possible reopenings which have been mooted. Whilst it is hard for even the most optimistic of railway enthusiasts to imagine that any of the lines covered in this book will ever be reopened, there is always the hope that parts of some lines, such as the superbly scenic Valentia branch, could be made more accessible for walkers and cyclists. If the political will was there and some funding could be found, a green highway made up of the remains of such routes in different parts of the country could still be created, providing a wonderful asset for both local people and visitors to the country. It would at least be useful if some official body could create a database listing those elements of the archaeology of Irish railways in the form of buildings, structures and stretches of abandoned trackbed which are still in existence.

I would strongly argue the case that these are now as important as historic buildings and remains from earlier times. Surely such structures as the remnants of the Owencarrow viaduct and those at Gleensk and Cahirciveen, the GNR roundhouse at Clones and the station at Bundoran Junction must have some value to those in officialdom concerned with the preservation of our history and heritage. This value should be recognised to stop them going the way of the LNWR hotel at Greenore. At the moment the conservation of such structures and artifacts seems to be left to local initiative, which is fine as far as it goes, but this part of our heritage deserves better treatment and should not be left to quietly crumble and fade away.

INDEX